Praise for *Pop Poetics*

"Andy Fitch's *Pop Poetics* shatters any blithe binaries that have crippled thinking about 20th and 21st century poetry; offers a refreshing cast of characters, which radically alters the playing field; and invents epistemological categories of aesthetic thought with use far beyond Fitch's thoroughly explored subject of Pop-inflected poetry. All this he does not only in service of Brainard (along with Bernadette Mayer, Eileen Myles, David Trinidad, Ted Berrigan, and worthy others), but also out of a desire—and an impressive ability—to "expand our sense of what we have heedlessly excluded from the realm of the poetically possible." Rigorous, full of delight, and utterly original, this is a game-changing work of scholarship."

— Maggie Nelson, author of *Women, the New York School, and Other True Abstractions*, and *The Art of Cruelty: A Reckoning*

"Andy Fitch's *Pop Poetics* is a brilliant and comprehensive study of the career and life of painter/collagist/diarist/poet Joe Brainard, who died of AIDS in 1994. It reflects his multifaceted brilliance, and suggests that he be regarded in a role central to many experimental traditions—not as someone on the outskirts of Pop or the New York School, but as a central figure who knew, in the words of Walter Benjamin, that the productivist writer's most urgent task "[is] to recognize how poor he is and how poor he has to be in order to begin again from the beginning." Brainard's quest for new beginnings, with its aesthetic roots in many conversations of his time and presaging many conversations to come, is Fitch's engrossing subject—always lucidly and rewardingly treated in this first serious and beautifully presented evaluation of Brainard's vast oeuvre."

— Maxine Chernoff, author of *Without* and *The Turning*

POP POETICS

REFRAMING JOE BRAINARD

ANDY FITCH

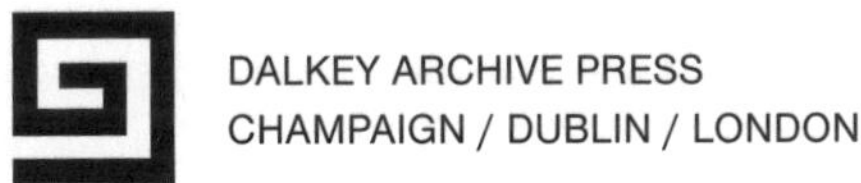

DALKEY ARCHIVE PRESS
CHAMPAIGN / DUBLIN / LONDON

Library of Congress Cataloging-in-Publication Data

Fitch, Andy.
Pop poetics : reframing Joe Brainard / Andy Fitch. -- 1st ed.
p. cm.
Includes bibliographical references.
ISBN 978-1-56478-728-6 (pbk. : alk. paper)
1. Brainard, Joe, 1942-1994--Criticism and interpretation. 2. Experimental poetry, American--History and criticism. 3. American poetry--20th century--History and criticism. 4. Poetics. 5. Pop art--United States. I. Title.
PS3552.R275Z58 2012
811'.54--dc23
2012004230

A version of Chapter One first appeared in *Interdisciplinary Literary Studies*, Vol. 12, No. 1 (Fall 2010), Published by Penn State University Press; and a version of Chapter Four in *Arizona Quarterly: A Journal of American Literature, Culture, and Theory*, Volume 68, Number 2 (Summer 2012), published by the University of Arizona.

Partially funded by a grant from the Illinois Arts Council, a state agency

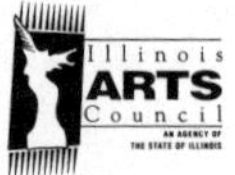

www.dalkeyarchive.com

Cover: design and composition by Sarah French

Printed on permanent/durable acid-free paper and bound in the United States of America

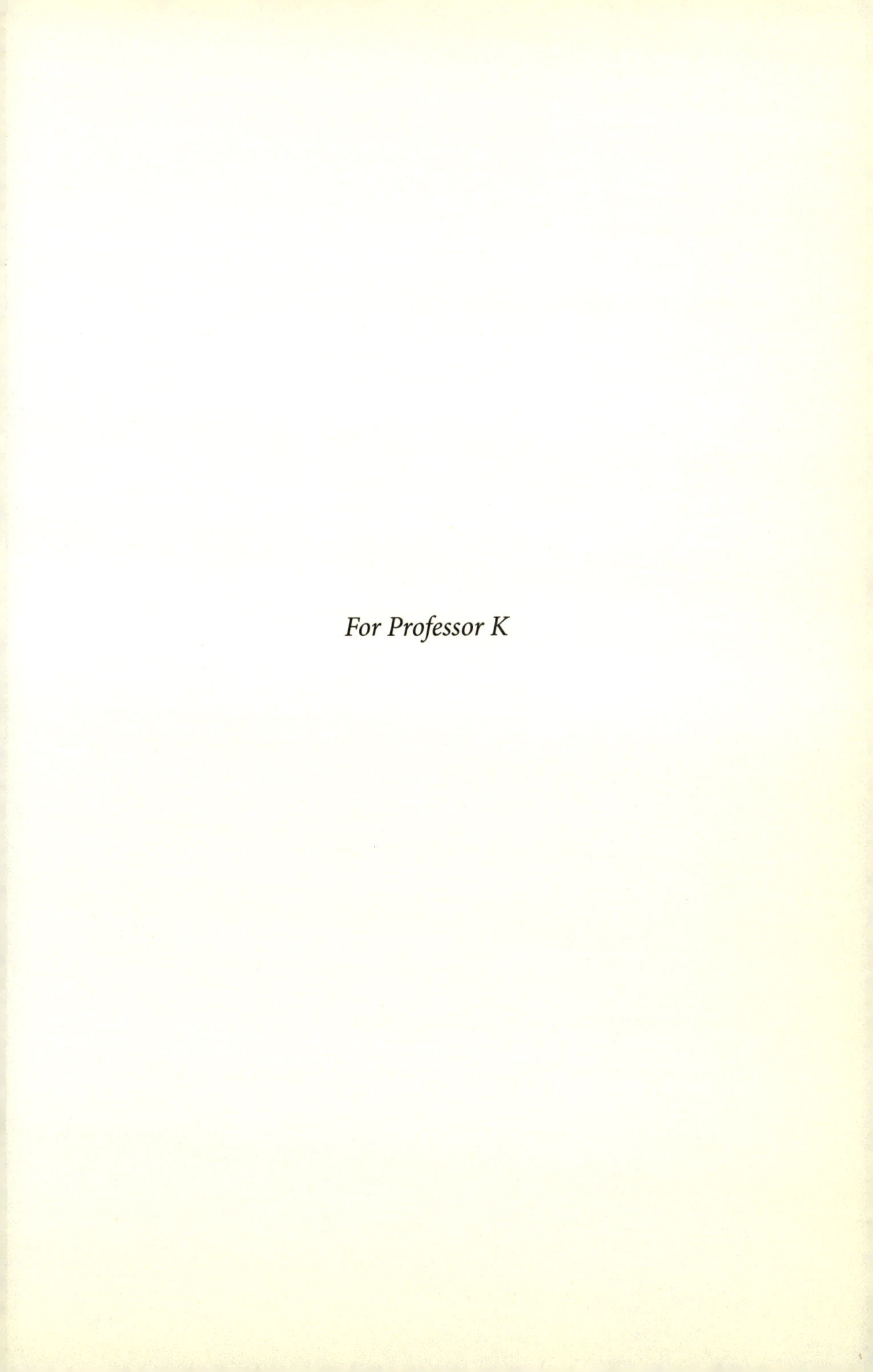

For Professor K

TABLE OF CONTENTS

List of Illustrations

Author's Note

A working draft of this project came about long before anybody except perhaps publisher Max Rudin could predict the impending arrival of *The Collected Writings of Joe Brainard*, put out by Library of America, and yet my basic premises remain unchanged. Apart from *I Remember*'s somewhat anonymous mode of success (as noted by Brainard advocates Ron Padgett and Paul Auster), texts such as *Selected Writings* and *Bolinas Journal* sat largely neglected in a few special collections and upstate library branches, with little critical momentum suggesting the possibility of a broader reappraisal. Moreover, whether lauded or dismissed by his contemporaries and subsequent audiences, Brainard's posthumous reputation (he died young of AIDS-related complications, during the years of malign neglect on the part of the Reagan and Bush '41 administrations) depended largely on quasi-mythic accounts of his disarming presence and endearing personal habits. Given the reductive accounts of New York School poetics then common among critics—exaggerated portrayals of an increasingly derivative coterie of name-dropping pranksters—this personalized account of Brainard's merits seemed likely only further to constrict his potential audience, especially among those scholars whose access to classrooms and course syllabi held the power to rehabilitate an overlooked poet's legacy.

For these reasons, my aim throughout this manuscript remained to place Brainard's poetic work amid a familiar, albeit interdisciplinary scholarly framework, as offered by early critical enthusiasts of Pop art. I hoped that my own exploratory book could serve as a prompt to any number of more substantial critical studies: of Brainard's pre-/post-Stonewall queer poetics; of the relationship between his artistic and literary production; of, in fact, his Fluxus-like resistances to institutionalized discourses of cultural authority and canonization. Needless to say, these heady hopes of mine, dreamed up during daily walks along the chintzy Midtown corridor between CUNY's Graduate Center and the New York Public Library, now seem a bit hubristic. Brainard is back, whether scholars care or not. Yet the existing narrative venerating Saint Joe, one developed with the best of intentions by friends as good as any poet can hope for, seems likely to stifle more far-reaching accounts of what Brainard's unclassifiable oeuvre can tell us about subsequent developments in the language-based, Camp-infused, appropriative, conceptual, New Narrative, and documentary poetics that have helped to shape our own poetic present. Within this context, I still can hope that the convoluted parallels and clunky phrasings of this manuscript help to open the possibility for sustained scholarly accounts of this too-long neglected innovator.

Joe Brainard, bashful/exhibitionistic I.Q.-test flop, defined himself as Not Intelligent. But Smart. Brainard's peers long ago proved astute enough to recognize the legitimacy of this declaration's latter half. It's still up to scholars to challenge the former.

ANDY FITCH
JANUARY 2012

POP POETICS

Introduction

Blowing up Paper Bags to Pop: Joe Brainard's Almost Autobiographical Assemblage

MARILYN MONROE AND KATY KEENE

Given that the scholarly discourse concerning postwar poetic experiment has marginalized collagist/poet Joe Brainard's literary output, I feel as much need to re-introduce this work as to articulate its broader critical significance.[1] Thus before beginning any extensive analysis of Brainard's writing, I will offer a quick sample of the Pop pleasures to be found there, will cite several entries from the first few pages of Brainard's best-known book, *I Remember*:

> I remember one of the first things I remember. An ice box. (As opposed to a refrigerator). (2)
>
> I remember when I went to a "come as your favorite person party" as Marilyn Monroe. (2)

I remember when a fish-tail dress I designed was published in "Katy Keene" comics. (5)

I remember playing "doctor" in the closet. (5)

I remember "The Tennessee Waltz." (6)

I remember Bickford's. (7)

So continue the memories: for 32 pages in *I Remember*'s 1970 Angel Hair edition, for 138 pages in the 1975 Full Court Press publication.[2] Yet I hope that even the short sample quoted above demonstrates why many Brainard advocates choose to dwell upon the poet's charming, true-to-life literary persona. At the same time, I want to suggest several limitations to any such biographical analysis (to a reading which remains, with rare exception, the only that Brainard has received). I want to reposition Joe Brainard as an avatar of interdisciplinary Pop aesthetics, as an experimentally inclined producer of a covert (perhaps closeted) abstract poetics—a project more concerned with the modular, mosaic-like deployment of prosaic fact and commercial figure than with literary defamiliarization in its most conventional (syntactical) sense.[3]

STARS AND LIGHT BULBS

In conjunction with the Berkeley Art Museum's traveling exhibition "Joe Brainard: A Retrospective," the literary annual *Pressed*

Wafer devoted a large portion of its 2001 issue to this protean artist/poet. Among the thirty-six contributors to "Hello Joe," two types of response predominate. Between them, one can trace a shift in posthumous presentations of Brainard: from prematurely departed friend (Brainard died of AIDS-induced pneumonia in 1994), to enduring poetic influence. My attempt to construct a critical vocabulary that can articulate what makes Brainard's quasi-autobiographical work so abstract starts here.

"Hello Joe" offers a balanced combination of inventive poems and elegiac essays. Yet to a fan of New York School poetics, personal testimonies by Brainard's closest companions might first stand out, if only because these pieces come from the anthology's best-established authors. Many prominent New York School figures (Bill Berkson, Tom Clark, William Corbett, Joe LeSueur, Ron Padgett, Lewis Warsh among them) provide first-person accounts of the Joe Brainard they knew so well. Taken as a whole, these recollections reinforce poet John Ashbery's claim (from the catalogue to a 1997 Tibor de Nagy retrospective) that "Joe Brainard was one of the nicest artists I have ever known. Nice as a person and nice as an artist" (*Selected*, 257). Corbett, for example, in his Editor's Introduction to the "Hello Joe" tribute, affirms that "Nice may be a surprising word with which to celebrate a late twentieth century New York artist, but it fits Joe Brainard" (2). Warsh and Clark deliver poignant depictions of Brainard's empathic presence and painstaking generosity. Given the overall frequency with which Brainard's beatific "niceness" gets mentioned throughout the *Pressed Wafer* compilation, one in fact may assume that the term does not fit this poet, so much as it defines him.

Readers thus introduced to Brainard's amiable reputation will be primed to note *I Remember*'s gracious foregroundings of the oft-overlooked non sequitur:

> I remember blowing up paper bags to pop. (125)

They stand less prepared, however, to apprehend Brainard's dexterous splicings of disparate semiological code:

> I remember "Last one to the corner's a rotten egg!"
> I remember "Go to jail—pass go—do *not* collect $200."
> I remember that George Washington Carver invented peanut butter.
> I remember blowing up paper bags to pop.
> I remember cartoon stars when someone gets hit over the head. And light bulbs for a bright idea. (125)

Here static conceptions of the poet's beneficent calm can obscure Brainard's decisive cut from one topic (one discourse, one subject-position) to the next. Within these five fluid entries, for instance, a preadolescent prompt turns into a Parker Brothers imperative, followed by a canned, split-second historical biography. Stories and voices appear, but without any of the ventriloquistic psychodrama of a John Berryman, or didactic orchestration of a T.S. Eliot. If a greater semiotic coherence occasionally does seem present (as when Brainard's final entry progresses from formulaic trope for traumatic dislocation [stars], to camp reification of creative thought [light bulbs]), we cannot confirm whether these rapid-fire statements imply stars or light bulbs above their own speaker's head—just as it remains unclear whether this sequence deliberately clusters around the aforementioned image of nihilistic creative-destruction, a paper bag blown to be "popped."[4] Interpretations arise, dissolve, as *I Remember* moves imperturbably ahead, or around, content to posit, like some paratactic branch of quantum physics, the presence of infinite parallel perspectives.

Of course the entries quoted above might appear to fall under the category Cute Childhood Memories, and to derive any cumulative force from a linear, associative logic. Yet I will argue that to ignore even this modest sample's contrapuntal punch is to deny the fugue-like dynamism which distinguishes Brainard's book (with its polyphonic account of postwar identity: of normative timidity and queer triumphs, of spontaneous insight and hackneyed representations; of vernacular and commercially driven speech patterns) from just any nostalgic take.[5] However straightforward *I Remember*'s syntax, its constant shifts in discursive register (sometimes subtle steps [stars to light bulbs], sometimes vertiginous leaps [Monopoly to George Washington Carver]) help to ensure that each reader's idiosyncratic assimilation of the poet's propulsive litany shapes this text's progression as much as any coming-of-age-narrative arc ever could.[6] However soft or banal Brainard's focus might seem, stars and light bulbs appear above our heads, too. "Saturation," in critic Marjorie Perloff's memorable phrase, "creates difference," and it is this construct of writerly differentiation amid a spare, serial, streamlined form that too often gets overlooked by biographical analyses of an *almost* autobiographical oeuvre like Brainard's (*Radical*, 215). Autobiography implies autonomous self-delineation, but Brainard's book—inverse of Andy Warhol's constraining, paint-by-number *Do It Yourself* canvases—asks its audience to provide the cohesive blueprint.[7] Prose-by-numbers (or by anaphoric, aphoristic entry) dictates that no matter the degree of intimacy present in retrospective paeans to this poet, the "I" of *I Remember* awaits forever to be described.

KINDNESS AND HONESTY

Again, the *Pressed Wafer* authors cited above do acknowledge an understated rhetorical complexity lurking within Brainard's oeuvre (especially in its coupling of restrained, repetitive design and accessible, extemporaneous tone).[8] Yet each contributor presents himself less as appraiser of the work than as witness to the man.[9] Even in brief evaluations of specific poems and collages, anecdotal references to Brainard's kindness and sincerity recur. To a Joe Brainard novice, these moving accounts might suggest the loss of not having been around to experience such legendary "tact, shyness and modesty" oneself (Corbett, "Introduction," 86). Still, "Hello Joe" tracks the consolation to be found in detecting Brainard's benevolent spirit as it emanates outwards from his "precise, sensitive . . . pleasing" art (86). *Pressed Wafer* readers thus can consider themselves introduced to "a man easy to greet" (86).[10]

I do not wish to extend this biographical reading of Brainard's output, either by affirming or contesting the pleasant character put forward posthumously by the poet's close friends. Yet "Hello Joe's" frequent emphasis upon benignant personality points toward interpretive conundrums common among responses to Brainard's (or, more generally, to New York School poets') quasi-autobiographical texts.[11] For even to remain, temporarily, within the limited set of "saintly" characteristics outlined above: Brainard's unflagging "kindness" proves difficult to reconcile with his emphatic "honesty."[12] Put more positively: the young Joe Brainard's dialectical approach to this kind/honest dynamic proves far more probing than any retrospective account produced by his peers.

While Brainard's cordial, compassionate touch might leave the present-day reader feeling well-tended (in 1980's *Nothing to Write Home About*, the poet even calls a tiny red bug "my friend"), his avowed pursuit of poetic "honesty" must have caused many contemporaries to feel exposed.[13] Already, for example, among *Selected Writing*'s earliest projects, Brainard cannot conceal a casually caustic indifference to conventional norms regarding family loyalty and/or professional discretion:

> April 27th is Kenward's birthday. May the 29th is my brother's birthday. My older brother, Jim, who lives in St. Louis. We aren't very close. I can't wait for summer. (50)

> I don't like to talk against art, as it is now, today, just because I don't, but something does bother me and that is the more intellectual minimal stuff. Like earth works, etc. I wonder who needs it? (51)

Such impolitic claims remain confined to Brainard's diary—appropriately enough, it would seem, were the poet not reading "Diary 1969" aloud to large audiences as he composed it. Yet, given this violation of the private/public protocol attached to journal keeping and poetic performance, even Brainard's most fleeting assertions pick up a confessional, confrontational charge.

To be sure, Brainard here emerges as no social dunce (unable to anticipate the context-specific consequences of his words), but rather as a deft delineator of myriad social milieux. Snugly situated among the overlapping circles of a buoyant gay urban culture, and of a close-knit poet/exile scene, drawn from provincial Middle America (in all its permutations) to cosmopolitan "Downtown" New York, Brainard need not worry about fraternal complaints getting back to his brother Jim. Moreover, given the increasing demographic disparities between New York's institution-sponsored art movements and its mimeograph-driven, self-publishing poetic enterprises, Brainard need not even fear his words getting back to Robert Smithson. Like Smithson's classic "East Coast/West Coast" spoof of the art world's reductive, divisive discourses, Brainard's "Diary 1969" can risk the occasional ungenerous aside, since its author ultimately remains less concerned with proffering didactic pronouncements than with sociologically tracing "where it's at."[14] Early into his literary career, Brainard already has begun to refine a convoluted, discreet/indiscreet performative two-step, easily lost in posthumous evocations of his impeccable tact. The self-parodic lightness of "Diary 1969's" laments ("We aren't very close. I can't wait for summer"; "the more intellectual minimal stuff. Like earth works, etc."), the camp comedy implicit within Brainard's staged self-exposures, wait to be unpacked by critical reflection—all but ignored by solemn appraisals of this timid poet's unstinting kindness.

But it is in 1971's *Bolinas Journal* that Brainard most pointedly probes the dialectical tension between kindness and honesty. For however anxious this poet might become about possessing "the power to hurt somebody without meaning to," he cannot help but criticize everyone in sight. (32) Much of this travel-journal's charm stems, in fact, from its author's aphoristic ambivalence toward the hospitable artistic community and impressive physical landscape he discovers. To offer but a brief (admittedly biased) summary of Brainard's trip—the poet prepares for travel:

> On way to airport. Cab driver wants to talk. I don't. Which seems to make no difference to him. (4)

stops off in San Francisco to see old friends:

> Lewis [Warsh]. I don't know. I love Lewis, but I just don't understand the "way back in there" position he's in. I don't know if he's stuck back there, or if that's where he wants to be. And I don't understand the "why" of either case. (7)

hears of impending arrivals:

> News that Ted Berrigan is coming totally zaps my mind. (Help) One of the nicest things about being here is not having a past to live up to. Or down to. I love Ted, but— (18)

surveys the new surroundings:

> This is a great place, Bolinas, but it isn't for me now . . .

> Bolinas is such a basic place. The land being so important. Survival seems to be the main issue.
>
> But for me life is still very much a matter of day and night. Can't think much beyond that. And I don't want to. (21)

appraises the professional and domestic lives of local luminaries:

> Bill [Berkson's] work is so clean and sincere. And if sometimes it seems to be trying too hard, "trying too hard" turns out to be a very nice thing. (23)
>
> Nice house they have, Robert [Duncan] and Jess [Collins], tho all that heavy furniture and stuff would drive me up the wall. (24)

carouses with his fellow boarders:

> Philip [Whalen], what little I was around him, was just too loud for me. (Talk) (27)

recalls those left behind in New York:

> Must admit (no, want to admit) that I really do miss Kenward [Elmslie] from time to time. (Like right now) There is no doubt in my mind that I really love him. And need him. But no doubt that it's not enough. (27)

provides the introduction for a poetry reading:

> When I was trying to do a portrait of Joanne [Kyger] I was surprised to discover that Joanne isn't really beautiful.
>
> But__She is. (30)

assesses the reading:

> If I wanted to be critical I could say that Bobbie [Creeley] was a bit "heavy" and that Joanne was a bit "bratty." (32)

muses on his future:

> Strange telephone call from Kenward last night. (Drunk and unhappy) No, not strange. Moving. Had me drunk and unhappy too. And wondering just how much longer I can take it. (32)

and prepares to return home:

> At four this afternoon Zoe Brown is giving a big picnic. Not sure how much I feel "up" to that. Too many people to say "goodbye" to. And I hate "goodbyes." (39)

Of course, along the way Brainard does deliver many appreciative details concerning the cultural/geographical locale, but this swift accumulation of critical commentary (within *Bolinas Journal*'s scant 48 pages) ought to preclude, I believe, any retrospective interpretation that essentializes Brainard's atmospheric kindness—while papering over his propulsive honesty.[15]

In fact, much more intriguing than survivors' nostalgic testimony to Brainard's infallible niceness is the author's demonstrated knack for producing unflattering portraits of close friends and peers, while still retaining their trust and esteem. For by 1971, the comfortable rhetorical distance that "Diary 1969" established between author and audience has been dramatically foreshortened. Whereas Jim Brainard of St. Louis most likely would not attend his brother's bi-coastal readings, *Bolinas Journal's* incidental characters seem bound to find their names in print.

However halting *Bolinas Journal*'s affections for Elmslie, for example, Brainard edits the project at Elmslie's summer home soon after ("Big breakfast. Worked on *Bolinas Journal.* Raspberries with sugar and heavy cream for lunch. Sun bathed. Did my exercises"), then publishes his record of this subsequent trip (containing further reflection upon "that telephone call Kenward made to me in Bolinas several weeks ago") as *Vermont Journal: 1971* (*New*, 14).[16] However qualified its appreciation for Bill Berkson's poetry (or, for that matter, for Berkson's girlfriend: "Suzan: very pretty. Sweet. And young. The only problem being I doubt if she knows what she wants yet"), *Bolinas Journal* gets published by Berkson's Big Sky Books later that year (*Bolinas*, 39). Here the timely appeal of Brainard's "honest" take—even for those most vulnerable to its purview—confirms the lasting value of these sketch-like projects more than any retrospective tribute to the poet's kindness could.

From our own era of supportive, small-press cultures, Brainard's camp-inflected theater of cruelty can offer comic vantage onto group dynamics pragmatically repressed by artists working within the proverbial Bolinas or Calais, Vermont, hothouse. At the same time, Berkson, Elmslie and Warsh's subsequent efforts to promote Brainard's legacy (each contributes, three decades later, to "Hello Joe") confirm the New York School's commitment to tracking abstract structures of interpersonal and intercultural exchange, even if/while appearing to emphasize self-congratulatory narratives or in-group patter.

No one should expect the intimate objects of Brainard's intermittent sting to unpack *Bolinas Journal*'s compressed conflux of ardent identification and ironic analysis with objective clarity. And it is for this reason that I soon will adopt the critical vocabulary art-historians have constructed in order to navigate the charged rhetorical depths of (ostensibly deadpan) Pop art. For though John Ashbery's paradigmatic account of Brainard's "incredible tact and generosity" assumes that, whereas "one can sincerely admire the chic and the implicit nastiness of a Warhol Soup can without ever wanting to cozy up to it . . . In the case of [Brainard's art] one wants to embrace the pansy," I cannot read 1971's sweetly sour *Bolinas Journal* without hearing in my mind Lou Reed's contemporaneous, Warhol-derived lyrics:

> Vicious
> You hit me with a flower
> You do it every hour
> Oh baby you're so vicious. (Ashbery, 258)[17]

Of course, pointed recapitulations of Brainard's unflinching honesty would provide no more comprehensive an account of his work's kaleidoscopic emotional palette than do tender depictions of the poet's invariable kindness. However "real" Brainard's testimonies and travelogues might seem, biographical homage—often strident (in its single-minded attempt to establish a compelling central character), or sluggish (bogged down by ambivalent, even-handed detail)—proves antithetical to the deft dialectical syntheses ("I love Ted, but—"; "'trying too hard' turns out to be a very nice thing"), and telescopic leaps in place and time ("Strange telephone call from Kenward"; "Big breakfast. Worked on *Bolinas Journal*"), that Brainard substitutes for conventional, character-driven narrative.

Thus in order to speed up my own biographical digressions, I have relegated to this introduction's appendix two further examples of how Brainard's diaries confound those reductive interpretive binaries (modesty vs. ambition; immediacy vs. artifice) reinforced by the poet's principal advocates. For now, I wish to leave this kind/honest continuum behind, not so that I can dust off New Critical discourse concerning the affective fallacy, nor to restage "the author's" death, but rather to treat Brainard's critical reception as a case-study of the broad neglect faced by postwar Pop poetics, by an interdisciplinary minded project to combine accessible icon and asymptotic structural-constraint—a motley amalgamation hard to contextualize amid contentious scholarly fields split by categorical distinctions between "transparent" confession and "opaque" language.[18]

JOTTINGS AND SONNETS

In their elegiac response to Joe Brainard's untimely death, first-and second-generation New York School stalwarts (Ashbery, Corbett, Berkson, etc.) celebrate a figure whose quiet, beneficent presence contradicts classic accounts of the ambitious artist.[19] But a second trend among *Pressed Wafer* contributions seeks not only to recall Joe Brainard the saint, but to invoke Joe Brainard the conceptually minded poet.[20] Whether or not these creative/uncreative homages offer an intimate depiction of their subject, each presents its own Brainardesque fusion of relaxed, vernacular record and austere, algorithmic design. If only to begin a much more lengthy demonstration of why, to my mind, Brainard's aphoristic assemblages and readymade meditations deserve to be valued as innovative poetic forms—rather than dismissed as diaristic fluff—I here will provide several excerpts from this latter type of "Hello Joe" tribute. For unlike the retrospective accounts of Corbett et al. (but like so many of Brainard's own projects), these accessible/elusive, prose/poetry hybrids remain almost impossible to summarize or to paraphrase—however "precise, sensitive . . . pleasing" their tone.[21]

Painter Darragh Park's "Jottings for a letter sent to Joe while he was in the hospital the last six months of his illness," for example, invokes the broad, inclusive attentiveness of Brainard's heterogeneous texts:

> "Greene St.", the sign, made me think about you
> The World Trade Center towers made me think
>   about you
> Walking down to SoHo crossing long evening
>   shadows made me think about you
> The word "Armani" in the *Times* made me think
>   about you
> Writing this makes me think about you
> Pansies always make me think about you—
>   so do peonies

A guy coming toward me in a white shirt, gray
    trousers, and an open, swinging black overcoat
made me think it *was* you (202)

Just as in many Brainard poems, "Jottings'" emphasis upon glancing minutiae need not preclude a sturdy, expansive construction (Park's comparisons continue for another 30 lines). Even after two full pages of diffusive detail, in fact, Park's piece only can end with an ellipsis—hinting that its author may not be finished in his tribute, may have generated enough commemorative momentum to make stopping impossible.

Surely Park seems as fond of Brainard as do his fellow *Pressed Wafer* contributors. Yet "Jottings" never allows for the type of quaint, anecdotal portrait outlined in this chapter's previous section. For beyond the poignant affects contained within its comparative catalogue, "Jottings" points toward the Brainardesque pleasures to be found less in simple, sincere descriptions than in subtle variation on a syntactical motif. Here fluctuations in tense and signature phrase ("made me think about you," "makes me think about you," "made me think it *was* you"); rhetorical shifts from metaphor (from allegorical objects substituting for Brainard, such as the "innocent" pansies he painted and, in John Ashbery's account, resembled) to metonymy (to artifacts contiguous with, but tangential to, Brainard's identity, such as the street-sign below his loft); procedural alternations between enjambed, sketch-like lyric ("Walking down to Soho crossing long evening / shadows") and cut text ("The word 'Armani' in the *Times*") all serve—along with the sudden appearance of a Brainard lookalike—to make this impressionistic inventory much more of an animated, interactive affair than most lists (Ashbery, *Selected*, 258). Park's propulsive attempt to assimilate all that stands present, all that can be connoted, all that might otherwise remain unsaid, resembles the insistent, omnivorous drive found in so many Brainard projects: from book-length works, such as *I Remember*, to swift, single-page statements like "Neck."[22]

But while "Jottings" recalls the perspectivist infinitudes contained within Brainard's pliant forms, David Trinidad's "Joe Brainard Pink" (a selection of twelve entries extracted from *I Remember's* 100+ pages) explores how a Brainardesque mode of attention also can yield the opposite result, can reduce an encyclopedic project down to one elemental trait:

> I remember pink dress shirts. And bola ties.
> I remember white buck shoes with thick pink rubber soles.
> I remember pink lemonade.
> I remember a picture of Jayne Mansfield sitting in a pink Cadillac with two enormous pink poodles. (166)

Pink may serve its distinctive part in regional costume (or in faddish accessory, specialized flavoring, Pop monochrome), but Trinidad's systematic return to this campiest of colors prioritizes the mnemonic charge found in a quasi-minimalist isolation of detail. Trinidad's piece thereby captures Brainard at his most redundant—resistant to normative code and to narrative progression. "Joe Brainard Pink" even transforms what had been prose blocks into discrete verse-units, thus privileging the lyric moment as it isolates its preferred imagery.[23] Still, Trinidad's kaleidoscopic compression of his subject's variegated pinks suggests that any obsessive inclinations latent within Brainard's literary output remain mysteriously wedded to the compulsive expansiveness echoed by Park (though the contemporary formula Obsessive Compulsive seems far too crude to describe this most "low key and offhand" of poets) (Corbett, "Introduction," 86).

Maxine Chernoff picks up on these paradoxical oscillations of scope and scale in her "Sonnet: Some Things I Miss About Joe." Within this elastic, fourteen-line construction, Chernoff confirms that even one of poetry's most compact forms holds ample room for a Brainardesque incrementalism:

> A golden tan
> Strawberry shortcake biscuits on July 4
> How he couldn't quite be lousy enough to lose to
> me at croquet
> Sending him books and getting ones back, including
> the great Barbara Pym (128)

As Chernoff's inventory accumulates without coalescing into pointed statement, its references to Brainard take on material heft, rather than accelerating towards climactic closure. Just as with a typical Brainard project, empirical fact fills in for dramatic flourish.

Perhaps, to the literary-historical ear, "Sonnet's" final two entries offer a Petrarchan twist:

An umbrella he lent me when he was too ill to
care about umbrellas

How his hair was graying towards distinction in
some future he never reached (129)

But a light, interchangeable poignancy present throughout the text ("How nice he smelled—was it Oil of Olay?") evokes the ambiguous effect of all-over design, rather than the elegiac thrust found in the sonnet-form's most famous lamentations. Chernoff's tribute thus reminds readers of Brainard the deft assemblagist, as much as of Brainard the tragically departed poet.

Along similar lines, Lee Ann Brown's "Joe Acrostics" recall the irreverent (yet loving) use to which Brainard put commonplace objects (himself and his companions included) throughout a resourceful career as illustrator/collagist/memoirist/aphorist:

Just
Over Bunches of
Easy Rain
And
Indigo
Noises,
Androgynous
Roses
Do it again (221)

For even as these acrostics foreground their schematic verbal distribution, the overlap of vertical and horizontal trajectories—of idiomatic ("Over Easy") and intercalated ("Easy Rain") phrases—convokes a modular monument to the endless possibilities of the pre-existing. Brown's method of "naming" Brainard recalls her subject's playful reorganizations of prefabricated data into allusive, yet inassimilable constructions: part John Cage mesostic, part Joseph Cornell dream-box.[24] Poetic analogue to Warhol's celebrity silk-screens, Brown's pixilated dilations upon J-O-E B-R-A-I-N-A-R-D commemorate this elder poet's prominent place within a post-Confessionalist, pre-Language poetics conspicuously aligned to Pop.

LYRIC AND L=A=N=G=U=A=G=E

Brown's acrostics (along with each of the other contributions quoted above) offer a tribute that depends upon constructivist assembly more than it does upon anecdotal recollection. Consequently, Brown, Chernoff, Trinidad and Park recall a somewhat different Brainard than do Ashbery, Corbett, Berkson, etc. The simplest method of distinguishing these responses might be to say that the former group channels Brainard's adventuresome literary "I," whether or not it addresses the biographical one.

This distinction would appear all the more apropos if Brainard's preferred type of poetic subjecthood proved easy to define. But it is the impossibility of achieving anything like a consensus account of the "I" in works such as *I Remember* that makes a Joe Brainard literary tribute so challenging in the first place. It is Brainard's characteristic mode of composition—an intricate arrangement of gnomic assertions and paratactic perspectives into apparently straightforward, autobiographical record—that can cause any analysis of the poet's "personality" to turn so misleading. For however closely Brainard's biographical and poetic "I's" might appear to overlap, the two remain no more identical than Brainard's *Ultra-New Realism Self-Portrait 1972* is to the (frame-escaping/frame-constructing) "eye" that conceived it [see Figure 1].[25]

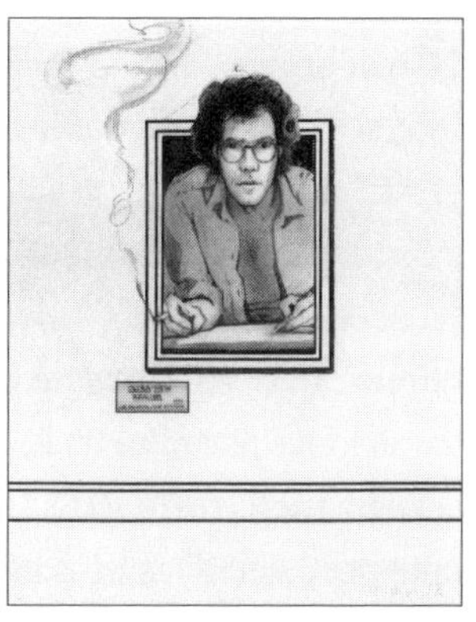

Fig. 1. Joe Brainard, *Ultra-New Realism 1972*, Self-Portrait
graphite on paper and collage, 13 x 10 1/2
Joe Brainard Collection, Mandeville Special Collections Library
UC San Diego

Thus, while I appreciate the charming recollections common throughout the scant secondary-literature on this poet, and while I respect the timely publication of intimate testimonials to a deeply missed peer, I believe that subsequent critics will have to choose between paying homage to one more poet-saint in the postwar pantheon, or to engaging Brainard's elusive "I" themselves. Extant assessments of Brainard's literary project (however praiseworthy for their promotion of his oft-neglected oeuvre) should be supplemented by studies that situate this artist/author's output amid broader aesthetic and intellectual trends. More generally, the rethinking of Joe Brainard poems ought to allow for the reassessment of an entire line of Pop-inflected poetry (of affect-heavy, conceptually rich texts by, among other poets, James Schuyler, Ted Berrigan, Eileen Myles, David Trinidad)—a corpus that remains marginalized (maligned even) by many progressive critics. Within this context, I will argue that the Brainardesque jottings, pink-poems and acrostics cited above deserve consideration not (merely) as idiosyncratic responses to private loss, but as canny extensions of a collective literary experiment.

The methodological questions posed by this less prosaic group of *Pressed Wafer* contributors can be summed up by asking what traditional lyric representation looks like once its full-bodied, well-modulated drive toward expansive, centrifugal scope (as extracted by Park) or obsessive, centripetal detail (as in Trinidad), toward a convocation of divergent scenes (as in Chernoff) or an intricate delegation of subdivided units (as in Brown), gives way to the twentieth-century's flattest aesthetic forms: collage, the grid, Pop seriality. The inability to address Brainard and his peers' work through prevailing critical paradigm need not prove an impediment to further study, moreover, once scholars note that Brainard's hybrid artist/poet career provides an ideal (if overlooked) point-of-reference for some of postwar America's most dynamic interdisciplinary exchanges.

Along such lines, any present attempt to situate Brainard amid the vanguard of poetic innovation seems likely to recall interpretive concerns posed by poststructuralist art-critics several decades prior: How (as Rosalind Krauss asks, in 1985's *The Originality of the Avant-Garde and Other Modernist Myths*) can critical discourse remain fluid enough to recognize when painterly gestures associated with "abstract" (as opposed to "representational") production become familiar figures, pictorial tropes—and in this sense turn conventional, symbolic? How (as Krauss's peers Benjamin Buchloh and Hal Foster explore in their examinations of quasi-realists Andy Warhol and Gerhard Richter) ought critics to respond when the most clichéd, content-heavy icons suddenly (Pop) become abstract?

To return to a literary-historical context, just when poets associated with the initial *L=A=N=G=U=A=G=E* publications begin to formulate their critique of the Romantic lyric's "referential" function (in 1977's "Politics of the Referent" symposium, for example), Krauss, Buchloh and Foster construct a critical dialectic that questions any abstract artform's ability to remain aloof from conventionalizing semiotic connotation— that problematizes any neo-formalist position which considers the axiomatic exclusion of "narrative transparency" a triumph of progressive aesthetics over commercial exchange, rather than a further reification of radical art's increasingly marginal status. Of course, the Language movement's attempt to purge poetry of its instrumental function quickly catches upon its own ideological snags. Astute poet-critics (such as Charles Bernstein in 1980's "Semblance," and Steve McCaffery in 1986's updated version of "The Death of the Subject") soon recognize the argumentative hazards of an avowedly anti-referential poetics. But little has been done to address, along the lines of Krauss, Buchloh and Foster, the converse critical possibility: the potential for a banalized, chatty, prose-like form to present a paratactic structure complex enough that any straightforward analysis of plot or character turns suspect, to the extent that readers may discern a new mode of poetic abstraction. Instead, during the decades between the Language movement's galvanizing assault upon "the referent," and sympathetic scholars' delayed acknowledgement of this position's rhetorical contradictions, a reductive conception of poetic experiment has become institutionalized into American PhD and MFA programs—a constrictive paradigm that leaves little room (theoretically, at least) for Brainard and his Pop-inflected peers.

REALIST AND RADICAL

Again, to treat Brainard's poems as autonomous texts, freed from any presupposition of authorial intent or referential specificity, would prove as reductive as to present these serialized, prefab constructs as unmediated, autobiographical documents. Yet a polarized critical discourse concerning "mainstream" (Confessional) lyricism and "radical" (Language) opacity has left little neutral terrain from which to consider hybrid forms that conflate first-person transparency *and* algorithmic artifice.[26] Nor do familiar analogies between postwar art and poetry help.

Scholars of New York School poetics long since have produced elaborate, interdisciplinary comparisons between the propulsive punch of an O'Hara poem and the painterly dash of a de Kooning canvas, between the asyntactical line of an Ashbery meditation and the all-over trajectory of a Pollock painting—most persuasively in

Marjorie Perloff's 1977 *Frank O'Hara: Poet among Painters*. Less well-researched, however, remain the affinities between New York School Poets' realist/readymade compositions (the collage-based long poems of James Schuyler and Lewis Warsh, the audio transcripts of Ted Berrigan and Harris Schiff, the constraint-generated and epistolary projects of Bernadette Mayer, the reinventions of oral epic by Alice Notley) and post-Abstract Expressionist developments in figurative representation and/or Pop appropriation (as found in the painted portraits of Fairfield Porter or Alex Katz, the silk-screened prints of Andy Warhol or Roy Lichtenstein).[27] Thus, even as pointed structural analogies between the classic Ab-Ex canvas and the prototypical O'Hara poem have helped to transform a coterie of supposed literary-pranksters into one of America's preeminent postwar avant-gardes, a comparative lack of interdisciplinary-attuned attention has relegated Joe Brainard and his peers to the margins of poetic scholarship.

In her 1997 addendum to *Poet among Painters*, Perloff, for instance, (praiseworthy for her prescient attention to a Poundian/neo-materialist vein of postwar poetic abstraction) not only outlines new avenues of synthesesiac scrutiny (the sound and vision of Language poetics), but summarily draws strict categorical demarcations between the divergent modes of rhetorical address ("sanctified" autobiography; "radical" asyntacticality) that Brainard's Pop-inflected experiments deftly conjoin (*xxv*).[28] By extension, Perloff's sustained assault upon a second- and third-generation New York School ethos—one that, in this critic's terms, captures "the O'Haraesque manner without the substance"—proceeds as if postwar poetics (like postwar art) had not long ago problematized classic abstract/representational dichotomies (*Painters*, 179).

"Manner" and "substance" prove quite difficult to disentangle, for instance, amid the affect-heavy, repetition-prone, simulacra-laden constructs of Brainard, Brown, Chernoff, Park, and Trinidad.

Still, my overall aim with this brief recapitulation of Brainard reception has not been to disparage Perloff's adventuresome scholarly pursuits, nor to deflate the buoyant goodwill of *Pressed Wafer*'s Joe Brainard *Gedenkschrift*, but rather to suggest the limited impact that nostalgic testaments to a "charming," "sincere," "saintly" poet seem likely to have upon prevailing critical paradigm.[29] The soft, somewhat vague terms with which Brainard texts often get described can make it appear as if any more rigorous investigation (along the lines of Perloff's *Poet among Painters* study) would obscure or upstage his "precise, sensitive, and pleasing" poems. Yet while a comprehensive account of Brainard's contribution to postwar Pop poetics will requires a closer reading of his published corpus, I hope already to have suggested why comparisons between Brainard's literary practice and post-Abstract Expressionist trends in visual art (the recycling of debased cultural artifacts; the construction of grid-like uniformity out of discrete, disparate elements; the serialized composition of a kaleidoscopic, quasi-autobiographical subject) provide as pertinent an orientation to this poet's experimentally minded project as do the poignant recollections produced by his friends.

SEITZ AND SCHWITTERS

While the main motive for my survey of recent responses to Joe Brainard's literary career has been to suggest that students of postwar poetics have much to learn from Pop-friendly theorists of visual art, I here feel compelled to admit that—in the particular case of responding to Brainard's eclectic output—art critics have fared little better than literary scholars. For as with the charmed, anecdotal accounts provided by Brainard's poet-friends, Brainard's strongest endorsements in the art-critical establishment (by contributors to *Artforum, Art in America*, exhibition monographs) tend to present this protean workaholic as a willfully minor figure. Why else, runs the argument, would the artist have chosen such an eccentric assortment of tacky trinkets for his sculptures, such kitschy content for his collages and drawings?

At best, sympathetic viewers tend to appreciate Brainard compositions for providing a witty foil to the macho rhetoric and genealogical self-consciousness of Abstract Expressionist and post-Ab Ex painting. Art-historian Robert Rosenblum, for example, assures us that, in Brainard's oeuvre, "there is no fretting about becoming a big artist with a capital B and A" (287). Carter Ratcliff concurs that "the art world's specialized concerns get short shrift" (74). Brainard's "own style has no antecedents" claims critic/novelist Edmund White (81). Yet a quick reconsideration of the art-historical record can demonstrate that Brainard had good reason to conceive of his work as part of a broader tradition in radical twentieth-century art, and as Pop-inflected complement to a collective postwar impulse—one whose alchemic arrangement of inert, utilitarian objects proved both as profound and as lyrical as any "Abstract" or "Expressionist" enterprise.

Most notably, as Ron Padgett's memoir *Joe* declares, by July 1963 the twenty-one-year-old Brainard had made his first assemblage. By August that year, "virtually all of Joe's work consisted of an assembling of parts, whether in 'collage-drawings,' assemblages or collages" (57). Nor did Brainard's sudden appetite for assemblage stand in pointed opposition to the staples of postwar art-critical discourse ("big" names, "specialized" concerns, historical "antecedents," etc.). For, as Padgett casually explains it: "The word *assemblage* had come into common use after an exhibition at the Museum of Modern Art called 'The Art of Assemblage' that Joe, Pat [Padgett] and I had seen together in 1961" (55).

While Padgett does not dwell upon that 1961 outing, his book's recurrent reference to "assemblage" illustrates this MoMA-exhibition's crucial importance to Brainard's artistic development.[30] If one had to categorize Brainard's heterodox aesthetic output over the prodigious decade soon to follow, assemblage seems the obvious point of reference.[31] From his black-cat-crucifix pencil holders, to his hand-painted flower cutouts, Brainard continually revisited and reinvigorated the assemblagist impulse (a form-minded dismantling and/or recombination of "common objects"—a reconfigured "realism" that nonetheless privileges abstract "relational structure") as culled by MoMA-curator William Seitz (Seitz, 9, 81, 24).

Of course, "The Art of Assemblage" did not have this galvanizing impact upon Brainard alone. MoMA's "Assemblage" exhibition helped to prime an entire generation of New York artists and critics for a rediscovery of early-twentieth-century European avant-gardism (most immediately, for Pop's renewal of Dadaist collage and Duchampian readymade).[32] Amid a parochial scene still largely devoted to Abstract Expressionism's "triumphant" sublimations, the sudden reappearance of Kurt Schwitters' motley MERZ-constructions, and Man

Ray's occulted household-objects, demonstrated that an artwork's dubious origins, idiosyncratic form and/or equivocal affect need not imply its unambitious nature.[33] As scholar James Boaden has recently described this Cold War thawing of art-critical paradigm: "Galleries long dominated by large abstract paintings and clunking welded sculpture instead sparkled with the poetry of everyday objects shackled together" (Boaden, 1). For a wide array of artists, critics and scholars, the "Assemblage" show "came as a revelation" (1).

In fact, a quick examination of Seitz's *Art of Assemblage* catalogue can confirm the breadth of intellectual and aesthetic debate circulating within Brainard's immediate purview, can suggest the narrowness, the sheer inaccuracy of any analysis that would present Brainard's work as disconnected from, or indifferent to, pressing art-historical concerns of his time. Seitz's expansive applications of the "assemblage" principle—in an era still dominated by the medium-specific critical discourse constructed by Ab-Ex champions Clement Greenberg and Harold Rosenberg—exert a lasting influence upon later descriptions of this hybrid form, and thus deserve citation:

> The term "assemblage" has been singled out . . . to denote not only a specific technical procedure and form used in the literary and musical, as well as the plastic arts, but also a complex of attitudes and ideas. (10)
>
> The term . . . would include all forms of composite art and modes of juxtaposition. In both French and English "assemblage" denotes "the fitting together of parts and

> pieces," and can apply to both flat and three-dimensional forms. (150)

Here a conceptual elasticity inherent to the assemblage ethos (Seitz's catalogue includes not only sections devoted to Cubist, Futurist, Dadaist and Surrealist objects, but also to texts by Mallarmé, Apollinaire, Gide) appears to invite Brainard's subsequent fittings-together of poetic "parts and pieces," just as Seitz's broader "complex of attitudes and ideas" (appropriation, collage, seriality) provides a fresh means of contextualizing New York School poets' heterogeneous, sloppy-seeming forms.

With Seitz's interdisciplinary scope in mind, for example, it is hard to ignore the fact that Brainard's quasi-autobiographical litanies look more like Vorticist manifestos (and read more like Rauschenberg combines) than like pieces of Confessionalist prose:

> I remember my first erections. I thought I had some terrible disease or something.
> I remember the only time I ever saw my mother cry. I was eating apricot pie.
> I remember how much I cried seeing "South Pacific" (the movie) three times.
> I remember how good a glass of water can taste after a dish of ice cream. (2)

Polar opposites, the sultry films and frozen treats of Brainard's post-war milieu take their respective place in this poet's "composite art"—intensifying, rather than canceling, each other amid *I Remember*'s deftly coordinated "juxtaposition." Protocols of shipshape masculine behavior aside, Brainard's torrential *South Pacific* relapse (cooled by an all-American dish of ice cream) finds its appropriate complement in a restorative glass of water. *I Remember*'s omnivorous progression (consumption) from screen memory, to screen image, to food-solid to liquid thus proves that this project's "complex of attitudes and ideas" can accommodate "both flat and three-dimensional forms."

Again, and briefly to recall *Bolinas Journal*—those constructivist "attitudes and ideas" that Seitz detects within the burgeoning assemblagist discourse can grant art-historical luster to some of Brainard's most inconsequential-seeming assertions:

> Right now I am out on the terrace in the last triangle of sun. Drinking a glass of rose [sic]. And wondering what I am going to <u>do</u> tonight. (22)

> At the laundro-mat. Sitting out in the sun. In a big wooden picnic table-like chair. (32)

Reposed, but alert, Brainard enjoys the teeming confluences of the American lawn ("the last triangle of sun . . . a glass of rose"), yet remains expectant ("wondering what I am going to <u>do</u> tonight"), waiting to be crowned king of Pop parataxis ("In a big wooden picnic table-like chair"). Taken as a whole (as one might peruse Schwitters' *Merzbau*, a cathedral-like "three-dimensional collage of wood, cardboard . . . broken furniture"), Brainard's scrap-suggesting entries (comics, sketches, maps, and photos break up a typical *Bolinas Journal* page) combine to prop a paper halfway-house, perched between classic conceptions of sculpture, picture, and poem—constructed along the elusive fault-line separating private (the terrace, the confession) from public (the Laundromat, the assemblage) space (Seitz, 50).

In subsequent chapters I will address ambiguities inherent to Seitz's elastic "assemblage" term, its partial overlap with "collage," for example (whereas assemblages include "composite" products of all sorts, among them monochromes and serial designs, collages rely more strictly upon the juxtaposition of unlike elements). For now, I simply hope to have established why any characteristic Brainard text can be read—like Schwitters' *Merzbau*, like Simon Rodia's labyrinthine *Watts Towers* complex (also showcased in MoMA's exhibition catalogue)—as one monumental, architectonic, art-historically attuned assemblage.

It is true that in the half-century since "The Art of Assemblage," critics have found much to contend with in Seitz's "rich, narrative tale" concerning a postwar "liberation of objects" and "reconquest" of the realist image (Boaden, 1; Seitz, 22, 81). Yet however quaint Seitz's declaration of an apocalyptic "New Realism" might sound today, his once progressive, paradigmatic text helps explain why—to an impressionable attendee of the "Assemblage" show, to a young arrival from Tulsa about to embark upon his own career as collagist/poet—the kaleidoscopic incorporation of clichéd content need never have suggested an indifference to abstract or avant-garde ideals.

To extend Padgett's point about "The Art of Assemblage's" impact upon Brainard, I here assert that the proto-Pop methods of Duchamp, Schwitters, and Rauschenberg helped this young artist to rethink the place of collage in literary experiment, to offer a compelling alternative to the two most prominent forms that appropriation art would take in postwar American poetics: the quasi-scholarly compiling of mythic, historical, and personal narrative (from Pound's *Cantos*, to Olson's *Maximus*, to Lowell's long sonnet sequences); and the splicing of dissonant syntactical units (from Robert Motherwell's *Dada Painters and Poets* anthology, to John Ashbery's *Tennis Court Oath*, to subsequent Language structures). Brainard's work tacks between the topoi of realist figuration and abstract design, between lyric and Language discourse—and demands a scholarly dialectic that can do the same.[34] Biographical sketches of the author and his peers need to be supplemented by pointed musings upon Pop art's anticipation of structural developments in poetry. For however indifferent to institutional precedent Brainard's (Schuyler's, Berrigan's, Mayer's, Notley's) poetic projects might seem, however flatly their prose-like Pop lyrics might fall, critics can do better than to treat such texts as mere objects arranged according to the laws of chance.

APPENDIX: GREAT AND CHEAP

As with Brainard's legendary kindness, his purported modesty must be contextualized amid a greater dialectical tension: between conspicuous personal reserve and striking professional achievement. Advocates of Brainard's "unassuming" literary corpus often understate the fact that by the time this then-28-year-old began work on *I Remember*, he had become one of New York's best-respected younger artists (a prolific collage-maker in his prime, and a close friend to many older, influential poets). For all his celebrated shyness and modesty, Brainard had good reason to feel proud of himself, and did not refrain from saying so—as these excerpts from letters to Ron Padgett make clear:

> At times like this I really know, though I rarely admit it to myself, I and the world are great and fucked. I'll never be happy or satisfied, I'll always be like this, so fucked . . . Will do great paintings, but will never do what I want. (32)

> I wrote a really good new thing ["Purple"] but it's really strange . . . I'm truly a genius . . . I feel super good . . . You might laugh if I say it, but for once you'll be wrong in doing so, [the new collages] are without a doubt *the greatest things ever seen* . . . They totally destroy all normal sense of perspective, logic, art, realism, etc. by way of contrast. (54)

> I am doing work now which surpasses me: I watch myself work in total amazement. And the results are no less surprising. It's all totally unexplainable. I'm not even myself anymore. (55)

> I am doing my best work right now. It is a garden but of a different sort (more abstract). It is the first thing I've done in years it seems that I am really nuts about. (133)

and—believe it or not—it gets better and better (my work) even though it becomes more and more of a torture to do it. (236)

Alas, it seems difficult to fit but this abbreviated selection from Brainard's many self-congratulatory appraisals into the straightforward account of a shy and modest artist (especially without undercutting Brainard's own evaluation of his work).

Even Brainard's intermittent self-doubt evokes the polar flare-ups of propulsive shame/ambition, rather than the consistent simmer of muddled, middling "humility." While fluctuations in personal estimate may be common among poets (and everybody else), Brainard's articulation of both extremes again ought to confound any reductive reading of his character. Brainard might not have been the only twenty-one-year-old artist to pronounce himself "truly a genius," producing "*the greatest things ever seen*"; but he was one of the slight few who could support these claims by getting his work placed on the cover of *Art News Annual* five years later, and certainly the only figure to progress from this enviable position to enrolling as a student at the New York Academy of Art in his early forties. Sympathetic critics, such as Brad Gooch, have made much of Brainard's early, "bodhisattva"-like renunciation of his artistic career.[35] For my own part, I would add that producing "better and better" work became "torturous" for Brainard due to the demands of unappeasable pride as much as to pangs of humility.

By extension, just as *Bolinas Journal* foregrounds Brainard's competing drives (toward kindness and candor) much more explicitly than do most posthumous evaluations of the poet, so *Self-Portrait: 1971* should long since have established the dialectical nature of Brainard's outward modesty:

Romantic

> I'm just sure I'm going to die young, which, ten years ago, was now. (*New*, 10)

Egomaniac

> I guess I must be an egomaniac, but, it's funny, I don't *feel* like an egomaniac. (10)

Conceit

> To tell you the truth, I don't think I'm as conceited as I have the right to be. (11)

As soon as Brainard decides to tell "the truth," the mild, self-deprecating tone so fondly recalled by the poet's friends picks up preemptory menace. For once, this closet-egomaniac stands prepared to break out his imposing credentials, and we readers edge closer to becoming humbled contestants in a bragging match (How many of us, as twenty-nine-year-olds, could claim Brainard's right to conceit?). Here unabashed honesty checks Brainard's more celebrated modesty—in the poet's own probing analyses, if not in subsequent statements by his supporters.

Along analogous lines, Brainard's artful orchestration of "simple," "spontaneous" language encounters greater skepticism amid the poet's own self-assessments than it does in posthumous appraisals of his work. Brainard rarely refers to his self-declared primitive style without acknowledging its manipulative intent. In *Bolinas Journal*, for example, the poet openly questions his affected naiveté:

> Our reading went very well I think . . . I was a bit embarrassed by my New York diaries. (So melodramatic)
>
> And I wonder about my being somewhat "primitive", and knowing it. And taking advantage of it.
>
> Is that being smart or is that being <u>too</u> smart? (24)

Yet even here Brainard cannot help "taking advantage" of the very conundrum he describes, deploying repetitive sentence fragments and faux-hokey typographical emphases to exaggerate his point.

Again, in an entry from *New Work* entitled "Wednesday, April 26, 1972," Brainard offers further instances of oscillation between camp self-criticism and convivial self-affirmation:

> Tonight (stoned out of my mind again) I just a few minutes ago found myself walking up and down (back and forth) in my loft, madly eating a bag of dried apricots, feeling sorry for myself (lonely and bored) not enjoying them one bit . . . I tried focusing all my attention upon

> the pleasures of eating dried apricots. And it worked! For a few minutes. But then I started thinking about how I should write all this down. As I am doing now.
>
> This strikes me as a bit "cheap" somehow, but—but I guess I just don't care.
>
> The "so what?" in me wins again. (57)

However cheap Brainard finds himself (stoned "out of his mind" just "a few minutes ago"), no apology ever emerges from this famously accommodating figure. Such bemused indulgence of an inner "so what?" hardly seems the sentiment of a saint.[36] Thus, once more, it is through the latter, reductive characterization that criticism emerges at its most repressed, and repressive: denying an obvious contradiction in the textual record (an interpretive conflict that ought to provoke refreshed analyses); diminishing the scope of an author for whom it appears to advocate; and concealing from younger poets a predecessor's most ambitious inclinations.

Chapter One

Personal/Perspectivist Space: Pop Poetry's Differential Calculus

POETIC SPACE

First, I will provide a brief sample of what I consider some of the postwar era's most abstract (epistemically pointed, form-minded) poetic texts:

> I remember how sad the "Jane Froman Story" was.
> I remember living rooms all one color.
> I remember green Easter egg grass.
> (Joe Brainard, *I Remember*, 35, 20, 31)
>
> First day of winter. Snow on the ground.
> Gathered in all the grapes. Snow on the hills.
> Full moon.
> Rooks resort to their nest-trees.
> Grey & sharp.

Earth-worms lie out & copulate.
Great rain. Hops sadly washed.
Ice bears: boys slide. Rain, rain, rain.
(James Schuyler, "Under the Hanger," 412)

I had an alibi for where I was on the night of August 28, 1985
    But the police still subpoenaed me to give testimony at
    A closed hearing
We hire someone else, a third party, to do our dirty work
When I was thirteen I got up on a stage in a house of God
    (so-called) & sang a song whose meaning the
  meaning of
    which was in the inflections of the words
A 2-ton trailer truck overturned on the Belt Parkway
  causing
    A tie-up on the Gowanus Expressway
I sing the emphasis of sound to convey meaning
  to somebody
I go to the store to buy some scallions
(Lewis Warsh, "Avenues of Escape," 42)

I really had no damn business there. I mean, why am I living with my ex-girlfriend and her new girlfriend, and *her* ex-girlfriend. How could that possibly be comfortable. I could be writing this from a jail cell. Funny, huh? Ted and Alice, before I left, said: "Out of the frying pan and into the fire, Eileen." I didn't know what else I could do. I flew, yes I did, up to Portland and Judy and Chris picked me up there. I was so ripped . . . (Eileen Myles, "Bath, Maine," 11)

> From Broadway to Hollywood, this is the fastest selling, most whispered-about novel of the year. *And no wonder!* Jacqueline Susann's VALLEY OF THE DOLLS reveals more about the secret, drug-filled, love-starved, sex-satiated night-mare world of show business than any book ever published.

*

> These tiny, whimsical characters were manufactured by Mattel from 1966-1971. Their name came from the combination of Little and Kid: thus the name Liddle Kiddles was born . . .

*

When Pugsley abandons his pet octopus to befriend a puppy, wear a Boy Scout uniform, and play baseball, Gomez and Morticia fear their child is becoming normal.
(David Trinidad, "Essay with Movable Parts," 13–14)

Of course, critics accustomed to esteeming experimental poems according to their emphasis upon literary defamiliarization, particularly syntactic (sentence-based) rupture, might beg to differ with the assessment provided above. Yet here I will demonstrate why, to my mind, Brainard's serial repetitions, Schuyler's kaleidoscopic collages, Warsh's deadpan juxtapositions, Myles's polytemporal anecdotes and Trinidad's appropriative assemblages deserve praise for constructing a pixilated, post-Romantic lyric "I," an "eye" that enables postwar poetics to assimilate the affect-heavy, perspectivally fluid simulacra of pop-cultural narrative.[37]

In what follows I will cite, as art-historical analogue to semiotics-savvy poetic experiment, the iconic immediacies and algorithmic displacements, the readymade, vernacular rhetoric and rarefied, medium-specific interventions of Pop art proper.[38] More specifically, I will present poet/collagist Joe Brainard as an ideal figure through which to track Pop poetics' affinity to Pop painting, as well as to place an oft-marginalized mode of poetic innovation upon mainline literary-historical trajectories: extending, for instance, from the dispersive designs of Whitman and Mallarmé to late-twentieth-century Language texts by Bruce Andrews and Steve McCaffery; from the fragmented faux-autobiographies of Rilke and Pessoa to the aphoristic meditations of Roland Barthes. For Pop poetics, like Pop painting, picks up its greatest critical significance, I will argue, not by brusquely dissolving commonplace distinctions between vulgar image and esoteric art-object, but by redirecting a modernist drive towards all-over composition into the motley realm of consumerist affect (TV-, radio-, tabloid-narrative included), into an alternately capacious and cramped postwar arena of monochromatic living-rooms and Gowanus Expressway tie-ups, of drunken romantic quartets and a "sex-satiated nightmare world of show business." Pop poetics adopts, I will claim, the oft-dismissed lyric subject as site for adventurous explorations of poetic space, and thus calls into question some of our era's most constrictive assumptions regarding the provenance of postwar experimental poetry.

SPACE NEGATIVE SPACE

Experimental poetry often gets defined by what it does not do. It does not offer a mimetic depiction of the world outside the text. It does not provide an unmediated, authentic account of existential personhood. It does not presume one-to-one correspondence between the poem's grammatical subject (its "I") and the author of the poem. In early statements by poets Charles Bernstein and Steve McCaffery, in recent recapitulations by critic Marjorie Perloff, Language poetics, for example, gets defined in contrast to "heart-felt," "expressive," "autobiographical" and/or "narrative-based" conventions.[39] McCaffery describes his peers' efforts as "counter-communicative" ("Subject," 3). Perloff places these texts in opposition to a resilient "Romantic paradigm" (*Differentials*, 153).[40] For more than a generation—from the late-seventies appearance of mimeographed L=A=N=G=U=A=G=E magazines, to subsequent publications on major university presses—Language poets and Language champions distinguish such work by emphasizing its departure from the mainstream lyric.

During an era in which the most popular poems depend upon a "bland cottage industry" espousing "neo-confessionalist, neo-realist" discourse, these distinctions prove crucial (Perloff, *Differentials*, 160-161). Yet, and as each of the astute authors mentioned above attests, proscriptive rhetoric adopted by early Language advocates remains prone to reductive opposition. One set of constrictive aesthetic criteria (poetry demands the discovery of individual voice, the reconstitution of what's most genuine in a person) easily can get replaced by another (avant-garde poetics *never* derive from vernacular speech, *never* depict personal experience, nor construct cohesive narratives). Poetic projects that systematically deploy accessible, affect-heavy sequences—if only further to confound the lyric-subject's authentic coordinates at a particular time and place—can end up summarily dismissed. Pop poets, for example (those, again, who assemble abstract compositional structures by stitching together mundane and/or mass-cultural points of reference), may find themselves mischaracterized as avoiding the essential intellectual/aesthetic debates of their time (mimetic "reference" vs. "opaque" design, etc.), rather than as probing paradigmatic repressions of the prevailing aesthetic regime. Pop poems may be disparaged as—in Perloff's analysis—"self-indulgent" Frank O'Hara knockoffs in which "the particulars don't add up," rather than read for what they can tell us about perspectival collage in postwar poetics and painting (*Painters*, 270, 183).

No more striking example of this far-from-benign neglect exists than the broader critical silence concerning Joe Brainard's literary output.[41] For while few postwar oeuvres remain in greater need of critical rehabilitation (of theory-minded supplement to an insular, biographical discourse that now dominates most references to the poet), few receive less attention (positive or negative) from the self-appointed guardians of avant-garde poetics. Among other attributes, Joe Brainard's poetry offers a charming, first-person account of quotidian experience, presented in an accessible, cliché-friendly idiom ("I remember packing up toothbrushes and washcloths and Crayolas [etc.] into individual Red Cross boxes for underprivileged children overseas"; "I remember rearranging boxes of candy so it would look like not so much was missing") and therefore, according to the proscriptive criteria outlined above, does not merit mention (126, 33).

But in an effort to problematize this negative definition of avant-garde poetics, I here will attempt to elucidate what a broad range of postwar poetic experiment *does* do. I will examine some overlooked affinities between Language's (celebrated) and Brainard's (undervalued) corpuses. By extension, I will argue that the conceptual overlap between a Pop-inflected poetics like Brainard's, and a "post-referential" enterprise like Language, only will become apparent once advocates of literary experiment directly address several interpretive conundrums (to simplistic form/content distinctions, for example) that Pop posed to art critics a generation ago. Within this art-literary-historical context, Brainard's quasi-autobiographical projects will provide an exemplary case-study for Pop poetry's construction of perspectivist space—a polyvalent rhetorical field as elastic as James Rosenquist's epic canvases, as emphatic as Andy Warhol's serialized silk-screens.[42]

PICTORIAL SPACE

Just as in our own, image-centric era, innovations in pictorial composition often precede those in poetry, so once-innovative approaches to art analysis still can help to update poetic criticism.[43]

Amid this present study of Pop poetics, I thus defer to art-historian Rosalind Krauss, a scholar whose poststructuralist readings of late-twentieth-century abstraction (Pop, conceptualism, and photo-realism included) define pictorial space as a "systematic play" of planes or perspectives—a braided "structuration of binaries" as difficult to envision as the differential code that Ferdinand de Saussure detects in language operations:

> But how would one paint Nothing? Clearly one approach is by means of that structure of oppositions in which each term of the oppositional pair is deprived to the greatest degree possible of its positive (limited, material, denotative) status. Meaning is not visualized as the result of the positive value of *a*, but only of *a*'s relation to *b*, and within this system, which Saussure characterized as one of "differences *without* positive terms," *a* is more accurately characterized as *not-b* . . . The Nothing that emerges from this play of oppositions, this structuration of binaries, is absolutely beyond picturing. (Krauss, 238)

A dynamic conception of pictorial space (of its "constant superimposition" of implied depths and empiric surfaces) allows a diverse range of artists to accommodate difference "without positive terms"—to foreground a "structure of oppositions" beyond any fixed, paraphraseable meaning (Krauss, 38). Here Krauss argues that an "insistence of figure/ground reversal" (from Cubist collage, to Abstract Expressionist canvas, to Pop silk-screen) has complicated our cognitive and perceptual experience of art, so that it makes less sense to isolate a particular object of description (a painting's ostensible mimetic content) than to track objects of discourse, "of *re*-presentation" (the kaleidoscopic values pictorial tropes pick up once placed in comparative relation to each other) (37). Such re-presentation does not commemorate specific "denotative referents," so much as it examines the "differential calculus at the very heart of the formal code of painting" (37). Image "A" loses its positive status (its ability to stand in for a real-world referent, such as a Campbell soup can), but "A's" infinitely malleable relation to "B" ("B" may provide an apparent copy of "A," yet advertise a subtly different flavor; "B" may combine ten such differentiated cans within a single canvas, etc.) allows progressive artists to keep refining (or reifying) pictorial construction at an ever-faster pace.

Most important to my present inquiry, Krauss includes within this "differential calculus" not only the classic dichotomies of pictorial analysis (light vs. shadow, color vs. line, etc.), not just the modernist bricolage of Cubism and Dada, but the "unpicturable" mesh of epistemic provocations at play in Pop art's scrappy assimilation of consumerist icons (a *canned*, clichéd Warhol silkscreen's pointed intervention into authenticity-minded Cold War discourse, for example). Confronted with "flat" postwar canvases, Krauss elects to treat such works neither (in her response to Abstract Expressionism) as sumptuous painterly surfaces, nor (in her treatment of Pop) as simplistic anti-art pranks, but as sites of writerly engagement. For as in Roland Barthes' epochal *S/Z* study, a text's polyphonic shifts of rhetorical register here prove more compelling than standard "form" or "content" considerations. Categorical terms (representation, abstraction) that tend to stand for positivistic values (for objective record, or autonomous field of aesthetic inquiry) themselves take on variable status amid Krauss's play of binary oppositions "absolutely beyond picturing."

Yet while Saussurian logic long ago presented a way for art critics to analyze "constant transpositions between negative and positive form," Saussurian rhetoric remains something of a reductive shibboleth within poetic debate—primarily used to distinguish mainstream verse from radical experiment (Krauss, 37). Within this literary-historical context, early Language discourse plays a prominent role not only in securing, but in circumscribing Saussure's impact upon poetic analysis.[44] More quickly, more competently than most poets and critics, Language advocates assimilate Saussurian principles, but rarely with the conceptual elasticity one finds in broad surveys of abstract/illustrational, original/readymade, painterly/indexical art by Krauss and her peers (Benjamin Buchloh and Hal Foster among them).[45] Thus even amid Language's timely assault upon stifling critical oppositions—"statement vs. style," for instance—constrictive interpretive paradigms persist: either (among neo-realist writing workshops) to treat confessional content as the preeminent matter of importance; or (among self-declared experimental circles) to pathologize "poetic reference" as a symptom of "mass aphasia" (Silliman, "Letter," 31). Between these poles, little room remains for a Pop poetics premised upon confounding any single-minded approach to first-person narrative.

But in an effort to broaden considerations of postwar poetic subjecthood, I wish to place Brainard's construction of perspectivist poetic space within an art-literary-historical context, to present

Brainard's quasi-autobiographical assemblages as a logical extension both of modernism's austere, all-over designs ("I remember watching my hair fall and accumulate"), and of Pop's accessible, iconographic images ("I remember bright orange canned peaches") (83, 36). For just as Krauss's Saussurian reading of Warhol silkscreens problematizes conservative critics' restatement of a "picture theory of art" (art as straightforward mimetic depiction), as well as the oppositional "either/or view whereby abstraction had to be subjectless," so this present chapter will question readings that treat Brainard's projects as mere autobiography, and/or treat systematic structural innovation as an arid, rarefied field left only to the most asyntactical of poets (249). Just as Krauss, in *The Originality of the Avant-Garde* and *The Optical Unconscious*, casts so-called competing aesthetic discourses (Cubist collage and De Stijl reduction; Suprematist construction and Duchampian readymade; "opaque" Abstract Expressionist surface and "obvious" Pop icon) as interrelated examinations of "the differential calculus at the very heart of the formal code of painting," I here will sketch the parallel pursuit of a differential calculus at the heart of twentieth-century poetic space (and, consequently, of post-Romantic subjecthood), a quest extended in the work of Mallarmé and Marinetti, McCaffery and Bernstein, Joe Brainard and James Schulyer.

PHYSICAL SPACE

At the apex of exultation—following thirty-seven exclamation points, and just after running "naked along the shore"—Walt

Whitman raises his "Song of Joys" to unprecedented heights:

> O to realize space!
> The plenteousness of all, that there are no bounds,
> To emerge and be of the sky, of the sun and moon and
> flying clouds, as one of them. (328)

With broken arms and burnt-out eyes (having denied himself the "well-endowed" spryness of "those who love whores," if only to pursue more ennobling passions and "embrace a cloud"), Charles Baudelaire, in the pose of an Icarus, plummets from proximity of "peerless stars" to unfathomed depths:

> In vain I've tried to find the pole
> And the equator-line of space.
> I know not by what burning gaze
> The wings were melted from my soul.
> (219)[46]

From either peak of post-Romantic transport, one can glimpse the frontiers of modernist poetic "space." For whether or not Whitman succeeds at comprehending the cosmos, whether or not Baudelaire fails to christen the abyss, each poet discovers fertile plains/planes of dialogic breadth and syntactical profusion. Whitman's immense assemblage of paratactic odes, and Baudelaire's vertiginous coda to tragic plot reversal, help to inaugurate a pursuit of "space" unbounded by the geographical confines of skies, moons, and suns. Any analysis of twentieth-century poetic space (that oft-traversed, rarely defined domain) would do well to begin with citations from such prescient forebears.[47]

But rather than puzzle through Whitman's oracular pronouncement, or catalogue ensuing efforts to realize Baudelaire's Icarian ambitions, I here will attempt to articulate a general principle by which to track some of the modern era's most compelling constructions of poetic space. More specifically, I will adopt a definition of poetic space borrowed from Rosalind Krauss's analysis of "pictorial space." I will start from the assumption that, just as modernist painters pushed beyond the established terrain of landscape, history-painting and portraiture—if only to construct abstract critiques of pictorial code—so the authors described below do not seek to make any grand lyric statement, but to reconfigure poetic space in accordance with evolving conceptions of literary subjecthood. Just as modernist pictorial space has less to do with any depicted (illusionistic) scene than with "the continual transposition between negative and positive form," so modern poetic space concerns itself less with colonizing Whitman's and Baudelaire's starry skies than with achieving virtuosic figure/ground reversal.[48]

Throughout the nineteenth and twentieth centuries, poetic space thus remains an amorphous, elusive concept: referring alternately to allegorical, typographical, semiological, and syntactical tropes. From *fin-de-siècle* reveries, to Futurist manifestos, to Pop-inflected projects, to language-centered writing, poets seek to encompass Baudelaire's "pole and equator-line of space"—and yet offer quite divergent strategies of poetic production. To varying extents, each approach defines poetic space as a discursive field constructed through the dynamic juxtaposition of differential units (metaphors, fonts, narrative and grammatical fragments, etc.). But whether this "field" resides in the symbolic depths, page design, perspectival vantage, and/or opaque phrasings proffered by a poem differs depending on the context. Poetic space, I will argue, proves as variegated, as multi-faceted, as the diverse manifestations of perceptual space advanced by modernist visual art.

Here I pick up the discourse concerning poetic space at the close of the nineteenth century, just when (to return to Krauss's art-historical sketch) proto-modernist painters rediscover the canvas surface as propitious site for new structurations of pictorial space. For much of the immediate post-Whitmanian, post-Baudelarian era, the paradigmatic model for poetic space remains similarly two-dimensional—analogous to the "space" constructed when differential elements (shapes, tones, etc.) get arranged on a painter's "canvas."

Perhaps the easiest way to conceive of this pictorial form of poetic space is to consider typographical arrangement. In his preface to *Un Coup de dés jamais n'abolira le hasard*, for example, Stéphane Mallarmé compares different modes of typographical space, from classical verse to avant-garde composition:

> The "blanks" in fact assume an importance, striking first: versification required them like a surrounding silence, to such an extent that a lyric piece or one with few feet usually takes up about a third of the leaf on which it is centered: I don't transgress against this system, but simply disperse it. (105)

Fittingly enough (given the empirically minded present in which "*Un Coup de dés*" first appears), poetic space assumes a material reality, one verified by the senses, and precisely measured ("a third of the leaf") by the appropriate professional authorities. In the wake of Baudelaire's Icarian crash, typographical dispersal allows for a slightly less dangerous (if no less spectacular) pursuit of "the pole and the equator-line of space." Thus even in this preface to one of the era's most radical poems, Mallarmé playfully claims to offer "nothing new except a certain distribution of space made within the reading" (105).

No elaborate analysis of this new poetic space seems necessary, moreover, since Mallarmé's own "'blanks'" assume such paramount importance—"striking first" as the reader scans the dispersed text:

JAMAIS

QUAND BIEN MÊME LANCÉ DANS DES
CIRCONSTANCES ÉTERNELLES

DU FOND D'UN NAUFRAGE

SOIT
que
l'Abîme
blanchi
étale
furieux
sous une inclinaison (105)

Baudelaire's raging abyss, Whitman's eternal plenteousness of all, retire "within the page, accepting the succession" of "slant" poetic paradigms (Mallarmé, 105). Mallarmé's bonsai-like dispersion of myriad forms and fonts confirms the modernist poem's domestication of mythological and geographical space.

In subsequent texts by Guillaume Apollinaire and F.T. Marinetti, this discovery of new poetic space corresponds to a radical redistribution of printed matter across the dispersed page, an incorporation and/or construction of arresting visual patterns, a dissolution of any strict distinction between content and form, word and image:

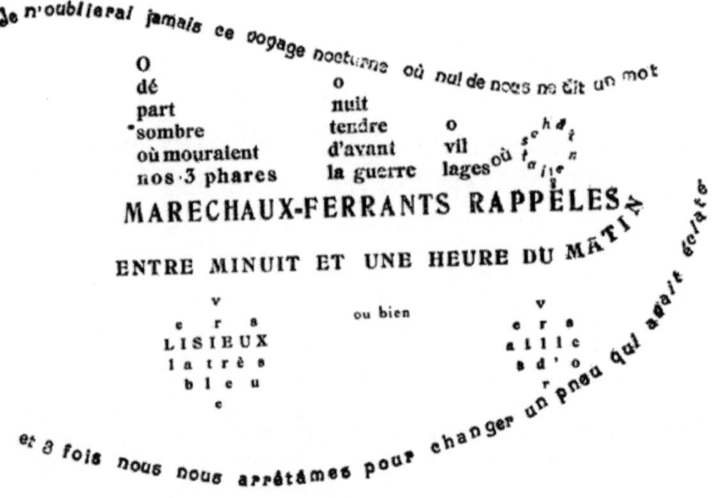

Fig 2. Guillaume Apollinaire, "La Petite Auto"

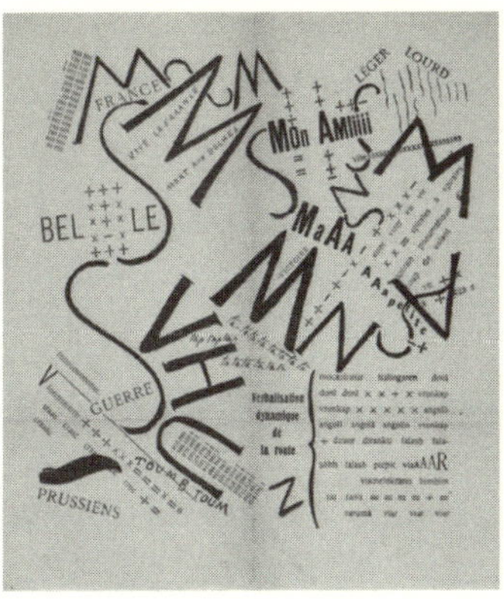

Fig. 3. F.T. Marinetti, "Après la Marne, Joffre visita le front en auto"

Along with Mallarmé, these latter poets help to close the ontological gap between art and poetry (quite literally: copies of their poems often get displayed beside contemporaneous collages and paintings, most notably, for this present study, as part of MoMA's proto-Pop 1960 "The Art of Assemblage" exhibition). Precursors (though not always appreciated as such) to New Critical proscriptions against the intentional and authorial fallacies, both texts can stand, like abstract paintings, as autonomous, self-sufficient objects.

Succeeding generations offer a diverse range of responses to this high-modernist conception of poetic space. Within postwar American poetics, for instance, works by Frank Bidart and Susan Howe exemplify (in quite different ways) the cultivation of poetic space through disparate typographical forms:

The FIST at the center of my chest

REFUSED TO UNCLENCH

until he and I, the furniture we
sat on, the room, the house,

THE VERY WORLD ITSELF

cracked apart,

then SELF-COMBUSTED,—

. . . self-consumed by our own self-contradictions.
(Bidart, "The First Hour of the Night," 189)

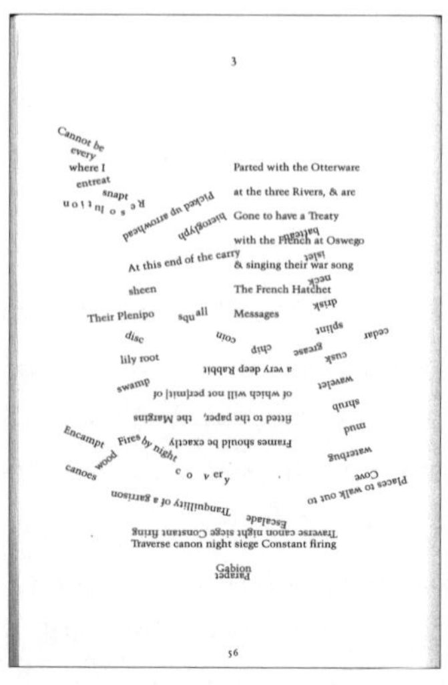

3

Cannot be
every
where I
entreat
snapt
R e s o lu t i o n
picked up arrowhead
hieroglyph
At this end of the carry
sheen
Their Plenipo
squ all
disc
coin
chip
lily root
a very deep Rabbit
swamp
of which will not per[mit] of
fitted to the paper, the Margins
Encampt
Fires by night
Frames should be exactly
wood
canoes
c o v er y
Tranquillity of a garrison
Escalade
Traverse canon night siege Constant firing
Traverse canon night siege Constant firing
Gabion
Parapet

Parted with the Otterware
at the three Rivers, & are
Gone to have a Treaty
with the French at Oswego
batteau
islet
& singing their war song
neck
The French Hatchet
drisk
Messages
splint
cedar
grease
cusk
wavelet
shrub
mud
waterbug
Cove
Places to walk out to

56

Fig. 4. Susan Howe, *from* "Thorow," from *Singularities*

Howe's "Thorow" often cites antecedent publications (Thoreau's letters, Melville's *Billy Budd*, Sir Humfrey Gilbert's *A New Passage to Cataia*) as source-texts—deploying words as physical found-objects rearranged into dynamic, crosshatched pattern.[49] Bidart's "The First Hour of the Night" assimilates various modes of typographical stress into the articulations of a more traditional lyric "I." Yet both projects refer back to Mallarmé's *Coup* (as Howe brusquely th[o]rows the "diced" text; as Bidart's clenched fist self-combusts), each providing a refreshing dispersal of mid-twentieth-century free-verse convention (the centered, "third-of-the-leaf" stanzas adopted by New Critical and Confessionalist poets). Complex metaphor yields to innovative typographical/pictorial construction. Symbolic image ceases and retires within the page.

SYNTACTICAL SPACE

Taken at a glance, Howe's topsy-turvy "Thorow" text might seem physically to restage Baudelaire's Icarian plunge. Yet "Thorow's" enigmatic individual lines ("At this end of the carry"; "fitted to the paper, the Margins") also point toward more recent attempts to map the poles of poetic space. For postwar innovators in poetic space often disperse grammatical or graphemic syntax. Following poststructuralist critiques of "instrumental speech," self-consciously radical poets seek, for instance, to "demystify the "referential fallacy of language" (McCaffery, "Subject," 2). The shattering of transparent lyric discourse into lexical or phonemic space (into novel crystallizations of linguistic signs and sounds) characterizes this more recent means of, in Mallarmé's terms, gaining a "literary advantage" by imposing "copied distance which mentally separates groups of words or words between themselves" (105). Poetic space can be dispersed not just across the page, but within the line, the sentence, the word, the syllable—again so that descriptive mimesis yields to a structuration of (now syntactical) binaries "absolutely beyond picturing."

If Howe's "Thorow" exemplifies this language-centered exploration of poetic space, early texts by Bruce Andrews, Barbara Barracks, Ray Di Palma and Steve McCaffery (here quoted from McCaffery's 1977 "Death of the Subject" essay) further confirm syntax's potential as site of "insistent figure/ground reversals":

> ca ja a th an ne sh th wa pe
> qu ci fo in ba wh vi re se th
> eu co st cu wo al su cr re re
> in ma vi si ba am ch qu an is
> (Andrews, quoted in "Subject," 14)

> stint grits
> darts file
> gratis ways to fit tins
> dapper angle
> ill apple
> sax wash
> max a phone
> (Barracks, quoted in "Subject," 3)

collides triangle lucid nap
broad wet exertion
        sift plunges
                    halo shallows
lean-to precocious
   trickle blade (Di Palma, quoted in "Subject," 10)

wlkt   sTdh

                              (FRPTO
        T
                         E

                    (fF)
                              Tts
(McCaffery, quoted in "Subject," 10)

From Andrews' polyvalent cut-ups ("th-an-ne"; "ci fo"), to Barracks' columnar combinations ("ill   apple"; "max   a phone"), to Di Palma's canny phrasings ("halo shallows"; "lean-to precocious"), to McCaffery's graphemic clusters ("sTdh"; [fF]"), new fields of poetic space emerge, new intra-syntactical meanings solidify as our attention to the "tautology of the signifier" (to the linguistic sign that remains a linguistic sign) sharpens (McCaffery, "Subject," 5). Poetic "reference"—that perennial lyric project McCaffery disparagingly compares to the "kind of blindness a window makes of the pane it is"—depends upon our habitualized response to "transparent" syntax, to a "motoric thrust of the word which takes you out of language into a tenuous world of the other and so prevents you seeing what it is you see" ("Subject," 2). Dissolving familiar, "motoric" bonds between letter and letter, word and word, early Language texts probe the differential calculus to be found amid atomized conceptions of syntactical space.[50]

Mallarmé's architectonic exclamations, Apollinaire's and Marinetti's charming or agitating pictograms, here give way to a collective effort "to centre language inside itself; to show the essential subjectless-ness a text might be; to stress the disemotional and dereferential possibilities of language as fragmentary, yet intensely direct experience" (McCaffery, "Subject," 2). Subsequent explorations of the line, the sentence, the paragraph, the chapter (in works such as Ron Silliman's *Sunset Debris* and *The Chinese Notebooks*, Lyn Hejinian's *My Life*, etc.) further expand Language efforts to construct, in McCaffery's more recent terms, "a textual space as a lettered surface resisting idealist transformation" (*North*, 17). Just as the dispersed page takes precedence in Mallarmé's compositions, so letters, words and the "subjectless" syntactical spaces that they shape interrupt Language texts' delivery of transparent scenes, narratives, emotions (classic lyric content). The liquid illusionism of referential discourse condenses into tactile poetic opacity.

Language's heterodox origins and variegated output deserve much greater attention than I can provide within this brief survey of twentieth-century attempts to chart the pole and equator line of poetic space.[51] For now, I simply desire to present this movement's early emphasis upon "the empirical experience" of a poem as an extension of Mallarmé's dispersed "distribution of space made within the reading" (McCaffery, "Subject," 3). At the same time, however, I wish to place McCaffery's pointed advocacy for decentered, "disemotional" Language praxis alongside Rosalind Krauss's contemporaneous critique of the conventional "either/or view whereby abstraction had to be subjectless—decoration—and a subject had to be a picture of something objective" (Krauss, 249).[52] Krauss's Pop-friendly art-historical account can help to steer critical explorations of poetic space back toward the oft-restricted realm of the affective poetic subject. Pop poetry's dispersion of quasi-autobiographical units eclipses, for instance, the integral lyric "I," even as Pop's perspectivist cohesion contests the "either/or view" affirmed by McCaffery and problematized by Krauss. Neither subjective in the Romantic sense, nor subjectless in McCaffery's terms, Pop poems overflow, as I demonstrate below, with dispersive subjectivities.

PERSPECTIVIST SPACE

Here I will track a less tangible realm of poetic space, one confined neither to the dispersed page, nor to the defamiliarizing utterance—two areas of particular interest to postwar poets and critics attempting to break from the New Critical treatment of texts as well-wrought allegories. Consequently, I will emphasize a mode of spatial innovation often ignored by scholars attuned to typographically and/or grammatically disjunctive poetries. For unlike the positivistic experiments of the bold shape-shifters and sentence-dicers referred to above, this latter realm of poetic space resides within the readerly imprint of a text. It concerns the affective movements implied by a poem, as much as our "empirical experience" of printed words and surrounding blanks. And given the phenomenological site for such novel configurations of "difference without positive terms," I here will grant this mode of poetic "distribution" the paradoxical name of perspectivist space. I will demonstrate that poetic projects which construct perspectivist space do not necessarily disrupt standard page design nor grammatical syntax, so much as they redeploy transparent-, plainspoken-seeming discourse amid serialized, mosaic-like compositions.

This association of the perspective and the composite may seem counterintuitive. A perspective typically gets classified as a subset—a single vantage on an overall scene, an engaged (or alienated) departure from Olympian objectivity. Perspectives derive from the individual subject, and thus suggest either an authentic or narcissistic (rarely an encyclopedic) account. Yet at least since Nietzsche's paeans to "intellectual perspectivism," perspectives also have been deployed as exploratory tools akin to poetic personae, as performative tropes for organizing unreadable infinitudes of random sense-data into provisional sites of inquiry. Rather than reify the text as autonomous object or pure syntactical signifier (as self-conscious descendents of Mallarmé and Saussure have done), Nietzsche (contemporary to Whitman and Baudelaire) calls on his peers to reinvigorate descriptive discourse through a dynamic assemblage of perspectivist space:

> From now on, my philosophical gentlemen, let us protect ourselves better from the dangerous old conceptual fantasy which posits a "pure, will-less, painless, timeless subject

> of cognition" . . . The *only* seeing we have is seeing from a perspective; the *only* knowledge we have is knowledge from a perspective. The *more* emotional affects we allow to be expressed in words concerning something, the *more* eyes, different eyes, we know how to train on the same thing, the more complete our "idea" of this thing, our "objectivity," will be. (*Basic*, 555)[53]

Instead of discounting mimetic reference, Nietzsche's elastic observatory mode demands as many "different eyes" (or "I's") as possible. Instead of pre-empting the experiential "blindness" that accompanies textual "illusionism," perspectivism constructs an additive objectivity (qualified by quotation marks). As this brief *Genealogy of Morals* passage—with its playful combination of pointed, prescriptive tone ("From now on, my philosophical gentlemen, let us better protect ourselves . . . ") and proliferating parataxis ("The *only* . . . the *only*"; "The *more* . . . the *more* . . . "; "our 'idea' . . . our 'objectivity'")—confirms, perspectivist texts depend upon carefully arranged composition, even when they appear to consist of compulsive utterance. As Nietzsche's exhaustive effort to complete his own "'objective'" account implies, perspectives serve not as truncated derivations from an organic totality, but as provisory place-markers for our (alas fictitious) conception of comprehensive wholes.

Modernist writers who choreograph such prismatic fictions into composite narrative (Rilke and Pessoa, for example, in *The Notebooks of Malte Laurids Brigge* and *The Book of Disquiet*) anticipate quasi-autobiographical perspectivist projects of the postwar era: from John Cage's story-based performance sequences, to Roland Barthes's incremental essay/memoirs, to Joe Brainard's Pop-inflected poetic fugues. For even at their most testimonial, these latter works do not presuppose the transparent lyric "I" so abhorrent to Language poetics, but rather disperse the speaking-subject across a potentially infinite field of supra-personal (perspectivist) space.

"PERSONAL" SPACE

To close this chapter, I will present a more extensive example of the rapid shifts in poetic vantage that I associate with complex constructions of Pop perspectivist space—again as demonstrated by several emblematic passages from Brainard's *I Remember*:

> I remember when I got a five-year-pin for not missing a single morning of Sunday School for five years. (Methodist) . . .
>
> I remember how much, in high school, I wanted to be handsome and popular . . .
>
> I remember an American history teacher who was always threatening to jump out of the window if we didn't quiet down. (Second floor)
>
> I remember my first sexual experience in a subway. Some guy (I was afraid to look at him) got a hardon and was

> rubbing it back and forth against my arm. I got very excited and when my stop came I hurried out and home where I tried to do an oil painting using my dick as a brush. (1-4)

For a thousand subsequent entries, the myriad depictions of Brainard's "I" pile up, never offering any essential indication of who this "I" is, but instead affirming Nietzsche's insight that even the most straightforward self-analyses requires "*infinite interpretations*" (*Gay*, 336).[54] Impervious to definitive characterization, Brainard's text deploys its "I" (its multiple "I's," it's Nietzschean "eyes") as diffusively as does any deauthored, decentred Language poem. However spare and simple any individual passage might seem, its strategic placement amid a greater network of comparable units soon eclipses consolidation of plot or comprehensive portrait—gently directing attention to the structural patterning that makes such unmediated-seeming testimony so perspectivally dense. Thus throughout his expansive project, Brainard's ever-promised "I" (loadstone of contemporaneous Confessional retrospection) remains propulsive agent of dispersal, rather than fixed object of scrutiny (here the poet's indefatigable, tautological "I remember I" constructions rival the "I am the man" of Whitman, the "I am I" of Jehovah). Yet out of this scattered/schematic anti-progression emerges a supple exploration of postwar popcultural subjecthood. Few literary experiments foreground such a convoluted relationship between incremental assertion and allover composition, between kaleidoscopic juxtaposition and cumulative affect.

Of course, one can treat Brainard's text as a more typical (if not exactly chronological) coming-of-age or coming-out story. A quasi-biographical reading of *I Remember* may argue that Brainard's "I" proves so authentic because his book presents the type of disarming contradictions that only could come out of real life: a man who has seen his mother cry once, over dessert, ends up gushing each time he watches *South Pacific*; a devout boy receives a Methodist pin and soon afterwards uses his dick to make paintings.[55] Brainard's story emerges through such poignant and/or comic complications of personal fact.

But far more dynamic contrasts appear as soon as we consider *I Remember's* perspectivist vantage upon its author-subject. For just when a sequence of idiosyncratic admissions seems to establish some sense of the poet's distinct, indelible character (detached son, serial *South Pacific*-goer), we find an austere, impersonal entry about how water tastes after ice cream, an affecting but equally generic passage about wanting to be handsome and popular, and then, offsetting this reductive mode, a competing desire to capture the decisive detail (the American history teacher's threat to jump from the second floor). Briskly, Brainard's "I" establishes its camp and constructivist, magnanimous and myopic, aesthete and quasi-autistic bents—and does so through insistent (if unobtrusive) figure/ground reversals.

It is this perspectivist variety in the presentation of personal/impersonal data, rather than any particular datum itself, which allows for an abstract but irreducible, engaging yet elusive "I" to appear (independent of self-aggrandizing assertion on Brainard's part). Like Barthes's desire for "the novelesque without the novel,"

Brainard offers the autobiographical without the autobiography.[56] Again like Barthes (especially in the theorist/memoirist/poet's aphoristic *Roland Barthes*, *A Lover's Discourse*, *Camera Lucida*, "Day by Day," etc.), Brainard elects to inhabit the rear-guard of the avant-guard—foregoing revolutionary gestures of typographical and grammatical rupture, if only to foreground dynamic structurations of perspectivist space. Just as Pop painting's assimilation of mass-cultural icon redirects the differential calculus of modern abstract art (fusing accessible image to esoteric epistemic intervention), so Brainard's canned "I Remember" phrase concretizes the double-consciousness implicit in lyric retrospection (and/or in postwar pop-cultural subjecthood), providing a readymade record of "ineffable" private experience, a re-presentation premised upon the absence of the thing described. Instead of offering unmediated access to authentic personal reminiscence, Brainard's book presents an amorphous "I" remembering such scenes—an "I" which, given its ubiquity, its requisite flexibility, remains the most indeterminate sign in the whole project.

Pop poetry's perspective-based reconfigurations of the testimonial subject thus can provide for a realization of "plenteous" poetic space (a "dispersal" of verse-form as elastic as Whitman's ecstatic odes and Mallarmé's poetic "distributions"). Pop perspectivism produces a "fragmentary, yet intensely direct experience" of rhetorical vertigo, a propulsive writerly pivot just as defamiliarizing as the "subjectless" opacities constructed through disruptive syntax. Obscured amid an era of contentious manifestos, Brainard's and his peers' less self-consciously combative (though no less timely) perspectivist projects deserve renewed regard as mosaic-like compliments to the Language critique of transparent poetic confession. For as postwar Pop art and art-criticism demonstrate, the twentieth century's differential calculus often proves dialectical: consistently overturning our conceptions of romantic and realist, abstract and representational, autobiographical and avant-garde form. Given this volatile context, it remains crucial for progressive literary criticism not to reinforce any one experimental discourse as the apotheosis of postwar poetic innovation, but again to expand our sense of what we have heedlessly excluded from the realm of the poetically possible.

Chapter Two

Serial Alternatives: Additive, Translatable, Productivist Poetry

SERIAL RECALIBRATION

In *Roland Barthes,* the self-scrutinizing critic recalls his youthful urge, playing "Prisoner's Base" amid the Luxembourg Gardens, to abstain from precipitous sally—to defer engagement until he could force a broad recalibration of the playing field:

> what I liked best was not provoking the other team and boldly exposing myself to their right to take me prisoner; what I liked best was to free the prisoners—the effect of which was to put both teams back into circulation: the game started over again at zero. (50)

Barthes, of course, carried this revolutionary (cyclic, at least) impulse into his intellectual career, regarding "the great game of the powers of speech" as but a more elaborate round of Prisoner's

Base, a perennial contest in which "one language has only temporary rights over another; all it takes is for a third language to appear from the ranks for the assailant to be forced into retreat" (50). The critic thus set himself one primary task, "to release the prisoners: to scatter the signifieds, the catechisms."[57]

Here I invoke Barthes's circuitously iconoclastic aims as justification for my own critical approach, a discourse that otherwise might appear quite defensive. For though elsewhere I attempt to define Pop-inflected poetry in positive terms (by probing the formal and epistemic affinities between, say, Joe Brainard's books and Andy Warhol's paintings), here I will not advance any "provoking," "exposing" argument, so much as I will employ Pop poetics as a "third language," a critical vantage from which to question paradigmatic binaries concerning realist and experimental verse, the neo-Romantic sequence and the postmodern serial poem. Parochial conceptions of poetic abstraction, and of poetic seriality, tend to peripheralize testimonial-tending projects by Joe Brainard, James Schuyler, Lewis Warsh, Eileen Myles, David Trinidad. Yet here I will position the above-named poets as central players in a "scattering of the catechisms." More specifically, I will treat Brainard's hybrid art/literary career as a prompt by which to introduce amid poetic scholarship any number of potentially destabilizing "third terms": among them modernist grid-painters' principle of "additive" composition, Pop artists' vernacular-derived "translatability" and Pop poets' peculiar mode of first-person "productivism." Rethinking Brainard's oeuvre thus will allow me to extend Barthes's metacritical form of Prisoner's Base—to play good cop/bad cop as I interrogate conventional distinctions between lyric and Language discourse, teasing out some oft-obscured affinities between these camps.

Astute period studies by scholars such as Reva Wolf, Daniel Kane, and Maggie Nelson already have begun to repeal the "temporary rights" that Language poetics (privileged discourse of late-twentieth-century poetic criticism) held over less-recognized means of innovation.[58] Wolf's 1997 text *Andy Warhol, Poetry, and Gossip in the 1960s*, Kane's 2003 *All Poets Welcome: The Lower East Side Poetry Scene in the 1960s*, and Nelson's 2007 *Women, the New York School, and Other True Abstractions*, have helped to recast New York School poetics (long overshadowed by reductive praise for John Ashbery, and/or Frank O'Hara) as a dynamic exchange among an ever-widening group of literary- and art-world participants: as a motley, multigenerational enterprise neglected due to its departure from, and contestation of, traditional publication strategies—a movement not lacking in experimental rigor, so much as awaiting scholars who take its myriad advances seriously. Epitomes of (to borrow poet/critic Wayne Koestenbaum's terms) "scrupulous scholarship," Wolf's, Kane's, and Nelson's cultural-historical excavations have expanded vastly the scope of primary-source material pertaining to postwar poetic experiment, even as they have made palpable the particular New York-based communities from which much of this work derives (Koestenbaum, *Warhol*, 222).

Given these successful syntheses of archival research, oral testimony, and curatorial retrospection, I believe that one means of further refining perceptions of the era hinges upon a return to early, influential critical assessments, both to consolidate our sense of foundational concepts from preceding decades, and to outline what even the most prescient critics *did not consider, did not recognize* as compelling poetic innovation—so to suggest how current scholarly parameters again might be expanded. Thus I begin this chapter by examining the paradigmatic conception of late-twentieth-century poetic experiment presented in Marjorie Perloff's forward-looking 1982 essay, "From Image to Action: The Return of Story in Postmodern Poetry." I then consider more closely one specific component of postwar poetic scholarship, the discourse concerning serial poetics (particularly as put forth by Joseph Conte's 1991 volume, *Unending Design: the Forms of Postmodern Poetry*). Regarding each respective critical text, I argue that a definitional emphasis upon the defamiliarizing and/or parodic postmodern poem has marginalized the contribution of an accessible, affirmative Pop-lyric vein, that a privileging of certain serial poets' "exquisite" output or "aleatory" ethos has impeded our receptivity to mass-cultural appropriations and quasi-indexical traceries. In both cases, I cite poet/collagist Joe Brainard's work (arguably one of the most postmodern, serially inclined corpuses of the late-twentieth-century), not only as example of a lamentably neglected oeuvre, but as a potential corrective to categorical distinctions (emotive/opaque, realist/abstract) that constrict our sense of the poetically possible. Nonetheless, I hope any criticisms I make of Perloff's and Conte's studies do not obscure the fact that my overall point is a complimentary one—to treat their innovative critical projects as source-texts equally pertinent to our conception of postwar poetry as any long-forgotten mimeograph stencil still to be discovered.[59] For as Focuault's epistemic inquiries have taught us, a revaluation of published (publicly proffered) suppositions that shaped an era's sense of "scientificity" can enhance our understanding of the past and present as much as any recently unearthed poem (42).

SERIAL DISTINCTIONS

Perloff's 1982 essay, "From Image to Action: The Return of Story in Postmodern Poetry," may not be her best known work, yet it still proves pertinent to present-day reconsiderations of postwar critical paradigm, especially to studies seeking to revaluate proscriptions against emotive affect and testimonial narrative. For here, Perloff's signature concern (which she later will describe as "our general inability to dissociate 'poetry' from the twin norms of self-expression and figuration") crystallizes into specific criteria by which to identify late-twentieth-century literary experiment (*Emergent*, 301). According to the standards "From Image to Action" puts forth, innovative work defamiliarizes the reader and/or parodies past poetic achievements. The return of poetic "'story'" brings with it the eclipse of lyric authenticity—both in Perloff's prescient pronouncement, and in many inventive texts soon to follow.

At the same time, however, Perloff's perceptive piece fails to acknowledge alternate means of innovation, largely because it conflates poetic experiment with explicit poetic critique, presuming that even the most adventuresome authors start with conventional, neo-Romantic tropes in their minds, then deviate accordingly. Pop poetry's deadpan mode of mass-cultural collage, for instance, can appear too cute and complacent amid this oppositional context. Yet I believe that Pop's appropriative interventions possesses their own particular virtues—strengths all the more timely, perhaps, two decades later, as Perloff seeks (in essays such as 1999's "After Language Poetry: Innovation and its Theoretical Discontents," and "Language Poetry and the Lyric Subject: Ron Silliman's Albany, Susan Howe's Buffalo") to moderate a combative exchange among fractious "realist" and "abstract" poetic camps. Along these lines, I here will examine what still can be gained by reading "From Image to Action," as well as how we might supplement the text's theoretical premises.

Perloff's piece swiftly establishes its literary-historical scope by tracing preexistent categorizations among a broad range of poetic forms—sketching, for example, Edgar Allen Poe's classic distinction between "short" (lyric) and "long" (narrative) poems:

> Behind this separation of the literary modes stands the Poe of "The Philosophy of Composition" (1846), who argued that a long poem is a contradiction in terms, for "a poem is such, only inasmuch as it intensely excites, by elevating, the soul, and all intense excitements are, through a psychical necessity, brief." For "long" and "short" we can easily substitute the words "narrative" and "lyric," Poe's point being that only the condensed lyric utterance—the cry of the heart—can produce the elevation of soul and "psychic intensity" that is the aim of all art. (*Dance*, 158)

According to Perloff's concise account, Poe posits narrative's inability to provoke "Longinian transport" (*Dance* 158). Baudelaire follows up on Poe's categorical pronouncement, pledging not to keep the reader's restive mind "'hanging in suspense on the threads of an interminable and superfluous plot.'" Plot becomes evermore passé, as modernist discourse prescribes a sharp distinction between "*poetry*, the lyric expression of personal emotions, and *prose*, the language of fiction, of the novel."[60] Instantaneous images and taut objective correlatives partition poetic "excitement" from narrative sprawl, and this restrictive legacy leads to a postwar context in which the title *Collected Poems* most often connotes "short lyrics or lyric sequences of an emotive or descriptive kind," an epoch in which testimonial accounts of the authentic and/or ecstatic lyric subject reflect poets' presumed duty to reconstruct privileged moments and peak experiences (159). Even when Robert Lowell and Adrienne Rich, for instance, do seek to demonstrate *gnosis*—the knowledge required to "narrate" (to tell)—they demur from plotting events in any third-person imitation of an action (the Aristotelian *mimesis praxeos*)" (157).[61] Late-modernism's "elevating" effects continue to demand the paring down of superfluous plot into lyric heart's-cry.

Yet according to Perloff's "From Image to Action" piece, this constrictive sense of genre proves less compatible with "the phenomenology of the present," an era in which consumer capitalism and mass-media saturation have eroded the boundaries of the "isolated speaker . . . in a specific landscape," meditating on his/her relationship to the "external world" (156).[62] Both the lyric and the narrative, in their most pristine forms, appear misplaced amid such a muddled, mediated context. Confounding reductive modernist distinctions, "story" thus finds its way back into the poem. Perloff cites, for instance, Frank O'Hara's "Poem (Lana Turner has collapsed!)," and John Ashbery's "They Dream Only of America," as proofs of story's partial rehabilitation, as peddlers of ebullient/enigmatic plot-lines—tales that no longer evoke the "full-fledged *mythos* of Aristotle" (161). According to the neo-Formalist (Shklovsky-, Jakobson-, and Bakhtin-derived) logic that shapes Perloff's analyses of late-twentieth-century literary experiment, O'Hara's and Ashbery's "'stories'" preclude catharsis, disappoint the reader's expectations and thereby promote poetic defamiliarization: "By frustrating our desire for closure ('Well, what *did* happen to Lana Turner?'), such 'stories' foreground the narrative codes themselves and call them into question" (161). The "Action" to which Perloff's essay title refers thus depends less upon any narrative arc, than upon postwar authors' redefinition of "poetic story" as a provisional "point of reference, a [playful] way of alluding, a source . . . of parody" (161).[63] The "Story" that Perloff's essay tells seems to confirm Poe's categorization of the long poem as a "contradiction in terms." Granted the significant tonal and formal disparities between Poe's "Annabel Lee" and O'Hara's "Lana Turner," for instance, these impassioned laments yet resemble each other in that neither appears amenable to book-length treatment.

In "From Image to Action's" latter half, Perloff does progress beyond the narrow confines of the short, "elevating" lyric. Yet the critic's emphasis upon postmodern parody of past poetic form remains unchanged. For as an extension of Ashbery's and O'Hara's puckish precedent appears perhaps "the greatest example of longer narrative poems" from the seventies, Ed Dorn's "epic of the Wild West," *Slinger* (164).[64] According to Perloff, *Slinger*'s eccentric progression and semi-coherent characters epitomize postwar play with poetic narrative—here by subverting the presumed "centrality of persons" to any self-respecting epic (167). Dorn's stated intent to "get rid of I" ("'I didn't want to have any truck with the first person singular'") corroborates Perloff's skepticism toward an inherited definition of poetry as "the lyric expression of personal emotions" (166, 158). Moreover, the ease with which *Slinger*'s "'flat'" characterizations yield to "learned allusions" anticipates avant-garde trends of the late-twentieth century (156). Already in Dorn's mid-seventies text, encyclopedic pastiche confirms language's ascendancy over "the threads of an interminable and superfluous plot":

> For the real hero of Dorn's poem is not, of course, the title character but language itself, the language of our time—an ingenious mix of scientific jargon, structuralist terminology, junkie slang, Elizabethan sonneteering, Western dialect, and tough talk about kicking a gorilla "in the balls." (167)

Here and elsewhere, Perloff's essay deserves reading simply for its wry, dexterous response to *Slinger's* virtuosic demonstration that any number of specialized idiolects can take "the form of parody" (158).

Yet is parody the *only* potential approach for a discourse determined to demonstrate that "*gnosis*" of the traditional type no longer seems attainable? Do the aphoristic assemblages of Nietzsche, Wittgenstein and Benjamin, the interstitial inquiries of Barthes and Derrida, not offer any alternate means of tempering and/or aestheticizing the "reflexive activity which seeks to 'know'"? (*Dance*, 157) Even within the (alas imaginary) confines of poetic innovation proper, need O'Hara's and Ashbery's detour from straightforward story, need Dorn's attempt to get rid of "I," and Language's distaste for lyric epiphany, devalue *all* postwar projections of "personal emotions"?

Perloff seems to argue so, at least in her constrictive predictions regarding "poetry of the future": "I would guess . . . a narrative that is not primarily autobiographical will once again be with us, but it will be a narrative fragmented, dislocated, and often quite literally non-sensical" (169). In this neo-Absurdist poetic future, as depicted by Perloff, the mere publication of fragmentary texts no longer will confirm one's status as radical experimenter, nor will the deliberate dislocating of fragmentary sequences; often these dislocated fragments themselves will need to estrange, to prove "quite literally non-sensical." If only to ensure a clean break from the ecstatic lyric moment, from the Confessionalist epiphany, poets will position the affective "I" as, at best, a laughable "anachronism in the poem" (168).

But alongside Perloff's apocalyptic conjectures, I wish to juxtapose Pop poetry's affective charms and quasi-autobiographical propensities. Joe Brainard's 1972 "30 One-Liners" piece, for instance, certainly calls into question the fixed, deterministic "*order* that a systematic plot structure implies"—offering a diffusive spread of discrete reflections (Perloff, *Dance*, 158; italics in original). Yet the poem's understated entries and paratactic pivots prove too disarming to qualify as classic lyric "parody":

> WINTER
> More time is spent at the window.
>
> SUMMER
> You go along from day to day with summer all around you.
>
> STORES
> Stores tell all about people who live in the area.
>
> WRITING
> Others have already written what I would like to write.
>
> TODAY
> Today the sky is so blue it burns. (*New*, 63)

Partnering the spare simplicity of the one-word title to the polymorphous complexity of the perspectival collage, Brainard's aphoristic project evokes most directly Gertrude Stein's "Tender Buttons" and Kenneth Koch's "Collected Poems"—with the obvious difference that Brainard's separate units could stand (however eclectic- or impersonal-seeming) as incremental components of a coherent, if kaleidoscopic, "I"-anchored monologue. Compared, moreover, to the chaotic plots constructed by O'Hara, Ashbery, and Dorn, Brainard's taut compendium makes for especially easy handling. In fact, it may be this blithe assimilability that best assures Perloff's indifference to the text. For whereas Dorn's protagonist-deprived epic foregrounds (in "From Image to Action's" terms) a "fragmentary," "dislocating," "non-sensical" anti-progress, Brainard's buoyant "I" strays just far enough from the Confessionalist center-of-gravity to preclude our unmediated identification with an authentic lyric narrator.

We still may identify, that is, with Brainard's modest, muted "I"; we just do not do so (as Shklovsky might put it) "automatically." Quite the contrary: recognizing the potential for a projective let-down (since Brainard's "I" appears but once, for instance, in the opening passage cited above, and only to admit its own authorial limitations), we read Brainard's text (*if* we read Brainard's texts) acutely conscious of autobiographical-narrative's reliance upon an unresolved erotic magnetism. For just as we may swoon before the attractive figure who obviously embodies "trouble," before the commercialized solicitation that only can end in consumerist self-deflation, so we get drawn into Brainard's "easy," accommodating text—nonetheless sensing that its matte pace precludes cathartic payoff. Edification, satisfaction only can come, we realize, through an appreciation for Brainard's deft "foregrounding of narrative codes," a focus rendered all the more keen for remaining outside Perloff's either/or (authentic lyric/parodic prank) schematics. "30 One-Liners'" thereby can pose manifold interpretive quandaries (Why does seasonal change from "Winter" to "Summer" propel the text to "Stores"? How do "stores" relate to the "stories" that they tell about people's lives? What influence do the stories of "others" have upon Brainard's own writing?), even if this piece never explicitly foregrounds the parodic ethos that "From Image to Action" attributes to experimental poetics.

Thus while Dorn's postmodern Western blows the lid off what Perloff elsewhere dubs a "bland cottage industry" of "neo-confessionalist, neo-realist poetic discourse," Brainard's minimalist meditations offer, at least to aficionados of equivocal affect (not the rare species one might assume—as Warhol's Pop successes confirm), an "elevating" pleasure far both from a sycophantic reverence for the self-aggrandizing lyric subject, and from a smug affinity to the self-mocking poetic parodist (*Differentials*, 161). Skirting either macho extreme, "30 One-Liners" seamlessly stitches the pleats of a soft, conversational, and/or epistolary camp, as anticipated by George Grossmith's *Diary of a Nobody* (1892), by Ivy Compton-Burnett's mid-century novels, and James Schuyler's *Alfred and Guinevere* (1958).[65] Even amid its most "simple" forms, alas, camp remains too complex a topic for my brief survey of postwar poetic scholarship to address. Suffice it to have suggested that Brainard's project innovates by deploying, rather than by discarding, banal topicality, colloquial diction and accessible affect. Such neo-dandyish attributes provide, in fact, for a delectable form of serial composition.[66]

For whereas Dorn's text deploys any number of ornamental gambits ("Homonyms, puns, nonsense words, coinages, archaisms, learned allusions, advertising jargon, a play on proper names"), "30 One-Liners" sticks to an unprepossessing prose-line as it systematically explores the potential relations between a poem's apparent paratext (here brusque, bold-faced captions) and its ostensible content (the "expressive" and/or "descriptive" definition each entry provides) (Perloff, *Dance*, 168). Symbiotic play between title and passage, moreover, stands in for global hermeneutic processes: for an all-over subjectivity indexed by (but never contained within) any number of discrete impressions; for a serial "story" so evenly distributed that it need not evince any formulaic structure. This serial-realist method allows Brainard and his Pop-inflected peers to achieve a diffusive, rather than disjunctive, mode of poetic abstraction.

Along such lines, one important distinction to make among serial enterprises is whether they construct (in the terms critic/curator John Elderfield employs for his contemporaneous *Artforum* essay, "Grids") "subtractive," or "additive" arrangements (52).[67] A grid painter may start, for example, by dividing preexisting canvas into modular units (along the "subtractive" lines of a Mondrian), or might gradually assemble a work's overall shape by combining individual bits into a composite, "additive" whole (as with Warhol's repeated silk-screens). I will elaborate upon this additive/subtractive binary in later chapters. But within the present context it seems clear that, however expansive in scope, Dorn's *Slinger*—at least as described by Perloff—pursues a top-down (subtractive) strategy, pushing its parodic prerogative along any number of discursive paths.[68] Brainard's tidy "30 One-Liners" concept, by contrast, can appear almost an afterthought, a well-rounded title granting retroactive coherence to the poet's propulsive (additive) catalogue. More generally, I would argue that parody (with its intentional, overtly critical thrust) leans towards the subtractive side of Elderfield's continuum, whereas camp (pursuing a less didactic pleasure in the erotics of fortuitous juxtaposition) inclines towards the additive.[69]

Of course, any categorical distinctions regarding such matters would prove as brittle as Poe's proscription against "the long poem."

Still I believe that progressive scholars' preference for disjunctive syntactical intervention has led to disproportionate emphases upon more-readily explicable (however "difficult") Language projects, at the expense of camp-inflected Pop compositions ("easy" texts such as Brainard's *I Remember*, James Schuyler's *Hymn to Life*, Eileen Myles's *Chelsea Girls*, David Trinidad's *Plasticville*)—not, as Perloff would have it, because these latter works sanctify "the 'natural,' the casual, and the unique speaking voice," but because their elastic deployments of additive affect remain beyond the narrow purview of late-twentieth-century critical discourse concerning the parodic and the defamiliarizing (*Painters, xxv*). In fact, given "30 One-Liners'" (and, as I will demonstrate, *I Remember*'s) adroit means of additive construction, Perloff's decision to treat "Slinger" as exemplar of 1970s experimental narrative can seem a form of critical containment: an elevation of the "dislocating," the "non-sensical," and, in these senses, esoteric, highly exceptional "'story'"; a valorization that obscures the utopian potential for Pop poems predicated upon a broadly engaging, yet epistemically provocative, post-lyric subject. I will return to this thought in subsequent pages, as I address Lawrence Alloway's concept of vernacular-to-the-vernacular "translatability," for instance, and Walter Benjamin's trope of textual "productivism." Here I simply hope to have demonstrated that a strategic arrangement of "ordinary syntax" and "anecdotal truth" can serve to critique the self-monumentalizing lyric "I" just as powerfully as does any deauthored, defamiliarizing construction. Perhaps no text confirms this principle more effectively than does *I Remember*—a first-person poem that diffuses its autobiographical subject across more than a thousand discrete entries. And as preparation for assessing *I Remember*'s algorithmic immensities, I must here turn to postwar "serial poetics."

SERIAL POETRY

In the 2004 publication *Joe: A Memoir of Joe Brainard*, poet Ron Padgett cites his friend's early-sixties "Gold and Silver and Purple Memories" text as antecedent to *I Remember*. I here quote from that ur-*I Remember* piece, as well as from 1975's complete edition of Brainard's most expansive poem:

> I remember Heinie the boy with glue on his fingers
> The fake silk hat / Green
> Sweetmeats, bonbons, Candy Kisses, and purple hearts
> I remember when a black night is truly black
> Her little girl madness
> And where are you Bronco Bill? (Padgett, 51)
>
> I remember shirt collars turned up in back.
> I remember Perry Como shirts. And Perry Como
>   sweaters.
> I remember duck-tails.
> I remember Cherokee hair cuts.
> I remember no belts. (10)

Comparing these two short samples, we can glean the significance in Brainard's mid-sixties foregrounding of poetic serial composition. For though both excerpts take adolescent mass-cultural identifications as their ostensible subject-matter, the latter poem complicates these associational/autobiographical tendencies—depersonalizing and decentralizing its retrospective "I," even as this abstract, anaphoric testimonial-subject gets raised to monumental importance (the column of vertical "I's" running down Brainard's page sometimes seems to blend into one immense majuscule).

Much as Warhol's serialized portraits celebrate their star's triumphant ubiquity (at the expense of his/her existential singularity), *I Remember*'s "I" transcends fixed time and place (at the risk of appearing schizophrenic, superficial). Much as Warhol's uncomplicated, ultra-realist depictions make for the most epistemologically advanced of compositions, Brainard's simple, straightforward syntax allows for the more nuanced poem. For whereas "Gold and Silver and Purple Memories" gushes with enjambed, anacoluthic, unpunctuated clauses, *I Remember* pulses with modular, matte "progress"—flat, perhaps, but peppered by any number of dexterous pivots (the transition from "Cherokee hair cuts" to "no belts" evokes, for instance, a slightly more liberated, counterculture-tending teen than does the random, conformist-seeming Cold War drift from "Perry Como sweaters," to "duck-tails," to "Cherokee hair cuts"). Retrofitting familiar fifties tropes of the "square," and of the "hood," Janus-faced Joe Brainard's polymorphous "I" points in two different directions: towards the gold-and-silver-and-purple sunset of nostalgic reminiscence; towards the utopian-charged dawn of Aquarian-age, Stonewall-era self-definition. Serial composition keeps this tacking between divergent attitudes and epochs elegant.

Yet few critics place Brainard among the postwar era's most innovative serial composers. And in order to explain why, I must launch another round of interpretive Prisoner's Base, so to demonstrate that scholars' longstanding neglect of Brainard's serial project hints at broader difficulties faced by all but the most self-evident (or, at least, self-declared) "serial poets" (George Oppen, Jack Spicer, Robert Duncan, and Robert Creeley among them). For though *I Remember*'s serial processes can be apprehended by a single glance, paradigmatic conceptions of the serial ethos exclude Brainard's "uncritical" reference to mass-cultural products (Conte, 14). According to scholar Joseph Conte's foundational study *Unending Design: The Forms of Postmodern Poetry* (1991), for instance, serial poets' devotion to "curvilinear and disjunctive" constructions precludes any straightforward testimonial record that seems "to bear too much the stamp of . . . reality" (23, 16). Conte's compendium of "postmodern forms" prioritizes works that "interpret phenomena" over those that "reflect them in an unmediated way," and, as a result, neglects (unjustly, I will argue) an entire line of Pop-poetic experimentation (17).[70]

Most important to my present revaluation of late-twentieth-century critical discourse concerning serial poetics, Brainard foregrounds additive construction through his employment of the anaphoric "I remember" phrase, and this incessant repetition leads to a very different form of serial composition than does the curvilinear and disjunctive "recurrence" Conte prefers to catalogue. Characterized as compulsive, considered less well-crafted than, say, those braided variations on a "matrix sentence" that comprise a typical Louis Zukofsky "song," Brainard's schematic structures remain too stubborn, too obvious to merit careful consideration from many an advocate of experimental forms (Conte, 210).[71] Yet to marginalize a grid-like litany such as *I Remember*, I will argue, obscures vital links between modernist painting and poetry, between early-twentieth-century serial statements and late-twentieth-century serial poems.

Due to spatial constraints, I here must neglect many useful distinctions derived from *Unending Design*'s "systematic typology" (assertive epic vs. meditative sequence, autonomous lyric vs. chance-propelled generative device, etc.), so to zero in on Conte's cogent, yet constrictive conception of the serial poem (1). In doing so, I seek, again, not to diminish Conte's contribution to critical discourse, so much as to complement his study of one now-canonized vein of serial poetry with my own emphasis upon a long-neglected, Pop-inflected praxis.

To sum up *Unending Design*'s presentation of postmodern serial poetics: Conte, like many adventurous critics, places postwar poetic experiment in opposition to a neo-Romantic, free-verse lyric—to a self-consciously plainspoken form, one reliant upon authentic testimony and organic coherence for its rhetorical effects. Unlike most experimentally minded critics, however, Conte, to his credit, provides positive indication of the specific aesthetic and epistemic objectives that poetic seriality seeks to establish through this departure from the lyric:

> The open form of the poetic series is defined by its limitless set of relations . . . The series . . . —with its aleatory and indeterminate qualities—thus supersedes in

its postmodernity an organic sequence that still hopes to discover an immanent form and a unity in creation. (15)

Whereas the "organic" lyric adopts a "metaphoric mode" (a rhetorical strategy premised upon affixing timeless truths in the form of local analogy and/or allegorical reduction), the "aleatory" series presents a "metonymic mode" structured by sets of tangencies (by an all-over design in which each "contiguous part [or metonym] on the poetic line, aware of its antecedents and consequent links, implies a contextual whole") (23). Amid such diffusive, mobile-like arrangements, the syntactic relations among separate units take precedence over the semantic meaning of any particular symbol. Thus, serial discourse (as emblematized by Oppen's *Discrete Series* [1934], Zukofsky's *Anew* [1946], Spicer's *Language* [1964], Lorine Neidecker's "Lake Superior" [1966], Duncan's "Passages" [1968-1987], and Creeley's *Pieces* [1968]) does not simply disallow lyric climax, but disperses itself beyond the possibility of definitive paraphrase. Poetic seriality reflects and demands an improvisatory assimilation of kaleidoscopic data, and points toward an ethos that Conte presents as inescapably tied to postwar "uncertainties and incomprehensibilities of an expanding universe in which there can be no singular impositions" (16). Given its apt response to our chaos-propelled episteme, the serial poem emerges (again, Conte's terms) as a "strictly postmodern innovation," a form that one can "easily distinguish" from its Romantic and modernist predecessors. (3)

Even within the late-twentieth-century context that Conte adopts as his purview, however, this critic's reluctance to acknowledge serial-realist innovation unduly restricts his scope. Conte's non-literary models of "postmodern" construction appear, for example, curiously dated: "Certainly postmodern poets deserve equal billing with the composers of serial music, the abstract expressionists, and the new novelists" (12). Here *Unending Design's* classification of serial score, Ab-Ex painting and *nouveau roman* as emblematically "postmodern" seems a generation off. Critics typically treat these enterprises as late entries into the modernist canon.[72]

But rather than quibble with Conte's comparative timelines, I prefer to broaden the field of inquiry, to theorize Pop-poetic seriality, first by noting several expansive definitions of serial aesthetics derived from the *post*-Ab Ex visual arts. Painter Mel Bochner opens his 1967 *Artforum* article "The Serial Attitude," for instance, by quoting philosopher Josiah Royce's turn-of-the-century *Principles of Logic* text—a work that answers its own rhetorical question "What is a series?" with abstruse mathematical delineations (Bochner subsequently compares Pierre Boulez' serialized grids of musical notes to the numerical chart that hangs in Albrecht Durer's 1514 engraving, *Melancholia I*) (28). Curator John Coplans' 1968 *Serial Imagery* monograph dwells upon Gertrude Stein's "Rose is a rose is a rose is a rose" formulation, placing this poet alongside philosopher Alfred Whitehead as "an early theoretician of Serial order" (7). Hal Foster, an art-historian whom Conte praises for separating "resistant" postmodernism from its "reactionary" twin, specifically associates the series (in his 1996 volume, *The Return of the Real*) with "industrial production, which more than any other force eroded the old orders of art, especially pristine nature" (62). Here Bochner, Coplans and Foster may themselves disagree upon the origins of serial composition; my point is simply that if art-critical discourse can address an historically and phenomenologically diverse range of serial sources, so can poetic scholarship, that if postwar painters and their champions seamlessly can cite Stein and Whitehead, experimental poets and their advocates can invoke compelling interventions by Pop practitioners and theorists—and, finally, that if literary critics pursued such lines of reflection, they would better appreciate an affect-heavy, serial-realist project like Brainard's. (For an analogous consideration of what the discourse concerning serial poetry stands to gain by expanding its historical scope beyond Conte's postwar-exclusive purview, see this chapter's Appendix.)

Thus contra Conte's axiomatic critique of "unmediated" form, I juxtapose critic Lawrence Alloway's deft, early (1969) response to Pop art's disarming mimicry of consumerist-era cultural production:

> Pop Art reveals constantly a belief in the translatability of the work of art. Pop Art proposes a field of exchangeable and repeatable imagery . . . Pop Art is able to share . . . themes from popular culture . . . Van Gogh would have welcomed it because he had the greatest respect for clichés, which he regarded as the authorized expression of mankind, a kind of common property that especially binds us together. (19)

Crucial to Alloway's "translatability" concept stands the fact that Pop innovation *need not foreground* its status as acute epistemic intervention, that Pop icons can move fluidly from vernacular culture, to fine-arts discourse, back to vernacular culture—just as the Campbell's Soup insignia drifts from depression-era grocery shelves, to early-sixties gallery display, to millennial Day-Glo "collector's" edition (distributed by Giant Eagle supermarkets).[73] Subsequent decades of Pop-friendly art criticism have taught us, moreover, that the "clichés" (the "common property") appropriated by Warhol, for instance, extend far beyond the superficial content of ads and tabloid images. For Warhol does not simply redeploy familiar icons (of soup, soap, Jackie, Liz, etc.), but redirects the projective gaze of the curious consumer—what critic Benjamin Buchloh describes as our "collective scopic compulsions: looking at the Other (in endless envy . . .) and the perpetually vanishing Self (in futile tokens and substitutes)"—toward its reflexive apotheosis (26). Dispensing with the art object's unique, handcrafted identity, the "translatable," interchangeable Pop product mirrors back our own, oft-mercurial sense of subjecthood. Whether or not this phenomenon falls under the narrow defamiliarization rubric devised by postwar poetic criticism, purveyors of Pop translatability certainly can be said, in Conte's terms, to "foresee implications" of technological advance, rather than to reflect those developments in an "unmediated way" (17).

To return to Pop-inflected poetry: *I Remember*'s most "common," "clichéd" element likewise appears not in any particular reference to "How Much is that Doggie in the Window?" or "The Tennessee Waltz," but in a serialized return to the stock "I remember" phrase. It is through this generic, nostalgic-hued construction, rather than through any quasi-populist content, that Brainard's "I" speaks most directly for "us."[74] For regardless of whether we remember Perry Como shirts (I don't), we employ the "I remember" tack; we adopt the myopic/encyclopedic vantage it implies, confirming (and conserving) our present sense of self through propulsive (if pre-selected) retrospection. Warhol's repeated silk-screens and Brainard's anecdotal sequences thus establish a crucial link between the serial painting, the incremental writerly-text and any number of oft-recycled tropes for collective cultural memory: from Lucille Ball sitcom, to Cold War *Life Magazine* cover, to Abraham Zapruder's footage of the J.F.K. assassination (all accounted for, incidentally, in *I Remember*). Along such lines, I subsequently will examine whether Brainard's Pop-poetic assemblage of "scopic compulsions" need necessarily reinforce the politics of stunned capitulation described by Buchloh.

SERIAL STATEMENT

Critical assessments of a postwar poetics premised upon Pop translatability must synthesize two "'familiar and unfruitful'" evaluative binaries—oppositions that, according to art-historian Hal Foster (here updating Walter Benjamin's 1934 "The Author as Producer" text), still plague our reception of art: "aesthetic quality versus political relevance, form versus content" (Foster 172). Brainard and his peers often get praised or dismissed, for example, for collapsing the interpretive distance separating complacent witness from compelling experiment. *I Remember*'s insistent assertion of a first-person poetic subject (just as "the author" suffers his historic demise) thus risks seeming retrograde. Yet Brainard, like Warhol, often appears most abstract when adopting realistic motif, most avant-garde when repurposing mass-cultural reference. For both artists dissolve distinctions between aesthetic quality and political relevance, between epistemic investigation and concrete form, amid (to quote Alloway again) "a field of exchangeable and repeatable imagery."

Within this context, Benjamin's own account of early-Soviet "productivism" (the realization of progressive political tendency through pragmatic transformations of the instruments of production, rather than sentimental amplifications of propagandistic message) can help to establish a critical dialectic capable of appraising postwar Pop (769, 774).[75] More specifically, reconsidering Benjamin's "Author as Producer" text can prompt us to regard Brainard's peripheral place among prevailing critical assessments as a sociological phenomenon, separate from any objective measure of *I Remember*'s aesthetic quality or political relevance. For Benjamin's timely, *entre-deux-guerres* observation that "the bourgeois apparatus of production and publication can assimilate astonishing quantities of revolutionary themes . . . without calling its own existence . . . seriously into question" seems just as pertinent in our present epoch—an era in which any number of self-declared radical, subversive, outlaw poetries find their way into scholastic purview, whereas Pop projects (epitomes of what Roland Barthes describes as a "soft" rhetoric) remain, alas, untouchable (Benjamin, 774).[76] Given, for example, Benjamin's acute delineation of a "decisive difference between the mere supplying of a productive apparatus and its transformation," I cannot help but wonder if academic discourse has more-readily absorbed "revolutionary" Language works, rather than "submissive" Pop enterprises, not because these latter projects lack historical resonance or aesthetic integrity, but because their insouciant, autodidactic air remains threatening to a salaried class of scholars and critics, disciplined readers whose singular skills shine forth in response to difficult texts (774).

Perused for profound content, probed for syntactic complexity, works such as "30 One-Liners" and *I Remember* do not seem to supply the institutionalized interpretive apparatus with topics worthy of its regard. Yet treated as "transformational" enterprises, as textual projects pitched to our intuitive appreciation for semiotic translatability, rather than to our trained esteem for argumentative nuance or artistic refinement, Brainard's poems flout the presumed need for professional intermediary between masterful poet and amateur reader. Thus while "post-referential" Language texts, for instance (ostensibly designed, in poet Ron Silliman's terms, to "return the poem to the people"), have, perhaps unwittingly, emerged as late-twentieth-century emissaries of an "'art of the difficult,'" claiming a respectable share of course time at elite universities, while pushing along toward broader canonization, Pop volumes such as *I Remember* remain, at best, quietly passed around (in Ron Padgett's and Edmund White's descriptions) thousands of classrooms across the country—most often the least-prestigious ones, from kindergartens to senior-citizens' workshops—folksy seminars filled with enthusiastic readers, blissfully indifferent to whom "first" uttered the fecund "I remember . . . " phrase (Silliman, "Letter," 34).[77]

Again, I by no means wish to disparage Language innovation. In fact, I soon will sketch how certain Language and Pop projects overlap, specifically through their productivist deployment of the syntactically simple anaphoric line. But first I feel the need to establish Pop poetry's productivist bonafides, both in accordance with Benjamin's own criteria, and in contrast to exclusionary praise for Language praxis. Most contemporary critics would agree, for instance, that Language discourse has taken up Benjamin's dictum (echoed by Barthes) to "eliminate the antithesis" between active artist and passive audience—both by precluding any automatized assimilation of author-determined content, and by drawing readers into the co-production of meaning (775).[78] Yet I would add to this standard assessment that Brainard succeeds at Benjamin's productivist enterprise even more so than Language.

For "The Author as Producer" summarizes productivism's "exemplary character" thusly: "first, to induce other producers to produce and, second, to put an improved apparatus at their disposal . . . this apparatus is better, the more consumers it is able to turn into producers" (777). And along such quantitative lines, Brainard's productivist mode appears better pitched to popular consumption. Whereas Language poems foreground productivism by complicating syntax beyond the range of "newer instruments of publication" (the morning weather report, for instance, and the nostalgic television sitcom), Pop poetics seeks to "use and learn" from these new forms ("the sky is so blue it burns"; "I remember duck-tails")—not to capitulate to mass-cultural banalities, but to "enter debates with them," serial inquiries concerning the potential for additive brio and epic, epistemic-minded translatability amid our own self-representations (Benjamin, 778). Thus, though classic Language texts certainly have spawned offspring, they lack *I Remember*'s distinctive ability to proselytize on productivism's behalf within the most unpropitious-seeming quarters, to turn lifelong "consumers" into reflective "producers" rewriting their own histories. Language poets embrace Benjamin's assertion that "An author who teaches writers nothing teaches no one" (777). But Brainard dramatically expands the base of available writers, picking up converts beyond the purview of both small-press poetic distribution and late-twentieth-century academic discourse.

Independent, moreover, from the modest pedagogical circumstances of Brainard's posthumous readership, this artist/poet's personal trajectory addresses what Benjamin dubs the productivist writer's most urgent task: "to recognize how poor he is and how poor he has to be in order to begin again from the beginning" (776). Feted as a rising art-world star, Brainard nonetheless, in his late twenties, redirects his prodigious serializing talents toward poetic production—thereby entering a verbal realm in which, *I Remember* tells us, its author long since had been deemed "below average."[79] Considered retrospectively, however, this inauspicious career shift does not suggest an impetuous break for Brainard, so much as it confirms the greater continuity of his productivist project. For the protean poet/collagist "begins again" in any number of ways. His mass-cultural appropriations and mnemonic-based assemblages foreground recycling as their modus operandi. His anaphoric and/or aphoristic structures substitute propulsive recalibration for progressive plot. His exportation of additive and translatable principles from Pop art to poetry exemplifies Benjamin's interdisciplinarity-affirming axiom that "the barriers imposed by specialization must be breached jointly by the productive forces that they were set up to divide" (775).

Due to spatial limitations, I only can offer fleeting reference to Brainard's "Ten Imaginary Still Lifes" piece—perhaps his quintessential "joint breach" of medium-specific painting/poetry constraints:

> Imaginary Still Life No. 1
>
> I close my eyes. I see a light-green vase. A very pale light-green vase. Right beside it sits something black. Something small. It is a small black ashtray. Getting smaller by the moment. Until—really—it is hardly more than—now—a tiny speck.
>
> Imaginary Still Life No. 2
>
> I close my eyes. I see white. Lots of white. And gray. Cool gray. Cool gray fabric shadows. (It is a painting!) With no yellow. By a very old man. (*Nothing*, 15–16)

"Ten Imaginary Still Lifes" confirms Brainard's status as a Benjaminian "revolutionary intellectual"; not, of course, due to any impassioned argument or explosive syntax, but because Brainard foregrounds his status as "betrayer of class origin," as art-world-aristocrat-cum-plebian-poet (a position he occupies with just enough camp flair, present in the sweet, slightly corny "I close my eyes" anaphoric phrase, to satisfy audiences craving more convoluted rhetorical vectors) (Benjamin, 780). Closing his eyes, Brainard nonetheless steps boldly toward the barrier separating pictorial impression from poetic abstraction.

Nor need this poet refer directly to the traditional still-life genre in order to achieve such effects. For Brainard borrows from contemporaneous visual artists (not just from their paintings and installations, but also from their printed texts) his solution to the post-Romantic hermeneutic problem of how to meld brief "excitement" and expansive scope—here through the construction of serial statements, perspectival assemblages in which aphoristic modules combine amid a polyvalent, mosaic-like whole. Within this context, I will close my chapter by demonstrating that the axes of postwar experiment and poetic seriality, as sketched by Perloff and Conte, obscure a vibrant line of serial texts published during the decade between Brainard's art debut and his Angel Hair Press *I Remember*.[80] First, however, I should provide a few representative excerpts from this shadow canon of serial statement:

> I am for an art that embroils itself with the everyday crap & still comes out on top . . .
> I am for an art that a kid licks after peeling away the wrapper . . .
> I am for an art that coils and grunts like a wrestler.
> (Claes Oldenburg, "I am for an art . . . ," 39-40)

> THE ORIGIN OF ART
> The discrepancy between physical fact
> and psychic effect

THE CONTENT OF ART
Visual formulation of our reaction
to life

THE MEASURE OF ART
The ratio of effort to effect
(Josef Albers, "The Origin of Art," 107)

There is just one participation, one perception, one invisibility, one insight.
There is just one edge, one framework, one ground, one existence, one fabric, one focus.
There is just one way, one side, one vision, one freedom.
There is just one problem, one task, one obligation, one struggle, one victory, one disciple.
(Ad Reinhardt, "There Is Just One Painting," 71)

Given these examples from Oldenburg, Albers, and Reinhardt, the broader affinity among postwar performance project, pictorial grid, and serial statement proves clear.[81] As with poet/collagist Joe Brainard's quasi-autobiographical texts, each artist's aphoristic assemblage provides the literal traces of serial composition—extracted from the repetitive procedures of abstract painting, and then transferred to the "quick graph" of the printed page.[82] In each case, moreover, anaphora serves as architectural basis for oracular/algorithmic utterance.

Again, compared to what Joseph Conte describes as Spicer's, Duncan's, or Creeley's "exquisite" and "ambiguous" stanzas, such compulsive, programmatic constructions may appear too effusive and/or argumentative to be taken seriously as serial poems (97, 111). Yet I hope to have demonstrated that, *pace* the broad generalizations and neat categorizations of late-twentieth-century academic discourse, the Boolean logic of poetic serial statement remains to be articulated: serial poetry contains (but is not encompassed by) the self-declared serial poems of Spicer, Duncan, Creeley, etc.; serial composition, in the textual sphere, includes hybrid works by poet/artists such as Brainard; postwar serial poetics, in the most expansive sense, incorporates pieces by authors otherwise absent from poetic discourse (Oldenburg, Albers, Reinhardt).[83] Amid these overlapping criteria, few aesthetic projects appear more timely than Pop poetics; few books seem more central than *I Remember*.

Nor need this centrality of Brainard and his peers detract from the significance of Language poetics. In fact, the additive model foregrounded by Brainard's anaphoric constructs can help refine reductive conceptions of how Language texts defamiliarize their audience (according to paradigmatic accounts, through the relentless deployment of difficult syntax). Along such lines, this chapter's last round of Prisoner's Base will allow me to demonstrate affinities between Language and Pop-poetic projects: under the sign of productivist anaphora, and in the wake of the modern art manifesto. For Language poets long since have recognized the potential energy to be found amid, as Charles Bernstein puts it, "varying kinds of referential vectors"—among them those of simple, streamlined locutions, arranged in serial pattern:

> Remembered a fragment of the king's face
> remembered a lappet wing

remembered eunuchs lip to lip in silent profile kissing
remembered pygmies doing battle with the cranes
(Susan Howe, *Hinge Picture*, 41)

Does it hurt? Is this too soft? Do you like it? Do you like this? Is this how you like it? Is it alright? Is he there? Is he breathing? Is it him? Is it near? Is it hard? Is it cold? Does it way much? Is it heavy? Do you have to carry it far?
(Ron Silliman, *Sunset Debris*, 105)

Let's just say that every time you fall you never hit the ground
Let's just say that when the day ends the night refuses to come
Let's just say that if all else fails you at least can count on that
Let's just say that a bird in the fist is better than a bird and a foot (Charles Bernstein, "Let's Just Say," 10)[84]

Such examples by prominent practitioners confirm that Language poets long ago expanded their conceptions of syntactical innovation, so to include all-over experiments with the anaphoric line, the aphoristic entry, and the anecdotal narrative. Moreover, within this present context, granted the preceding example of Brainard's anaphoric, insistent "I," it becomes all the more apparent that each "subjectless" Language poem cited above invokes a paramount "you" (Howe employs imperative clauses; Silliman adopts the interrogative form; Bernstein couches an implicit "us" amid his conditional contraction "Let's"). However deauthored, or post-referential, each text thus builds a quasi-narrative momentum through its anaphoric redeployment of the interlocutory-subject. Through their mobile appeals to an amorphous "you," these syntactically streamlined projects conjure a collectivist-minded agency, and hearken back to the modernist manifesto (John Cage's "Composition as Process" piece, for instance, contains roughly one-hundred consecutive questions), thereby providing a productivist mode dependent less upon syntactical rupture than upon the multivalent vectors of serial statement. In turn, Howe's, Silliman's, and Bernstein's repeated emphases upon "you" point toward a manifold-subject lurking amid Brainard's own additive, anaphoric lines—the plural-tending "I" of the perspectivist manifesto, as inherited from Whitman, and picked up by modernist, Pop, and Language texts throughout the twentieth century.[85]

Of course, the postwar affinities among Brainard's, Oldenburg's, Albers', Reinhardt's, Howe's, Silliman's, and Bernstein's statements still might seem superficial (suggesting, at most, each over-extended author's occasional dependence upon a hasty, anaphoric figure). Yet it is just this modular mode of construction that unites the hermeneutic acuities of painters' grids to the sprawling scope of serial manifestos—and that grants simplistic-seeming forms, such as *I Remember*, much of their intertextual and art-historical resonance. For even during the prewar era, serial composition did not remain under the exclusive provenance of Suprematist and De Stijl canvases, but extended to serial statements by Futurists, Dadaists, and Surrealists:

> 1. *It's stupid to write one hundred pages where one would do*, only because the audience through habit and infantile

instinct wants to see character in a play result from a series of events . . .
2. *It's stupid* not to rebel against the prejudice of theatricality when life itself . . . is for the most part *antitheatrical* . . .
3. *It's stupid* to pander to the primitivism of the crowd, which, in the last analysis, wants to see the bad guy lose and the good guy win.
(F. T. Marinetti, Emilio Settmelli and Bruno Corra, "The Futurist Synthetic Theater," 193)

[Dada] is like your hopes: nothing
like your idols: nothing
like your political men: nothing
like your heroes: nothing
like your artists: nothing
like your religions: nothing
(Francis Picabia, "Dada Cannibalistic Manifesto," 317)

THERE ARE motor and aeronautics shows
THERE ARE beach games
THERE ARE beauty competitions in the air
(Salvador Dali, "Yellow Manifesto" 367)[86]

However disparate in tone or content, each text quoted above posits the assimilatory prowess of the anaphoric line—and thus anticipates Brainard's all-encompassing poetic catalogue. For just as *I Remember*'s litany could easily absorb many of Oldenburg's "I am for an art" entries ("I remember wrestlers coiling and grunting . . . I remember licking after peeling away the wrapper"), so Brainard's signature phrase could tactfully refurbish the Futurists' scornful "It's Stupid's" and Picabia's nihilistic "nothings" ("I remember writing one hundred pages when one would do . . . I remember wanting the good guy to win"; "I remember heroes . . . I remember religions"), or help to humanize Dali's detached notations ("I remember beach games . . . I remember beauty competitions"). In any case, just as anaphoric structure allows Marinetti (et al.), Picabia and Dali to channel their potentially scattered surveys into taut, prophetic-toned compendia, so Brainard's omnipresent phrase grants his diffusive-tending composition a melded, multitudinous solidity beyond the sum of its detailed parts.

Along such lines, I conclude by contending that the modest "I" of *I Remember* resounds (however calmly, however quietly) with the assertive "we" of a preceding generation at its most voluble:

> We are proud, handsome and predatory.
> We hunt machines, they are our favorite game.
> We invent them and then hunt them down.
> (Richard Aldington, Henri Gaudier-Brzeska, Ezra Pound, William Roberts, Edward Wadsworth and Wyndham Lewis, "Our Vortex," 343)

> WE DENOUNCE the total lack of youth in our youth
> WE DENOUNCE the total lack of decision and audacity

WE DENOUNCE the fear of new events, of words,
of the risk of the ridiculous
(Salvador Dali, "Yellow Manifesto," 370)

Again, the predatorial and denunciatory "we's" cited above differ drastically from Brainard's all-affirming "I." Their combative tones suggest the serial statement's ability to conjure a collective premised upon opposition, exclusion, aggression (thereby anticipating, for instance, the chummy, chauvinistic, "There it is, brothers," of Charles Olson's "Projective Verse" manifesto). Brainard, by contrast, transforms the adversarial pack instinct of the Vorticists' plural-subject, and the pompous royal "We" of Dali's text, into a perpetual, polyvocal re-configuration of self—most often with that self presented as Wittgensteinian "limit" amid the greater social body:

> I remember the first time I saw myself in a full length mirror wearing Bermuda shorts. I never wore them again. (29)
>
> I remember socks that won't stay up. (47)
>
> I remember starched dress shirt collars. (122)
>
> I remember being talked about as tho I wasn't there (130)

Taken at first glance, *I Remember*'s retrospective trend-spotting may seem to typify the amateurish, solipsistic, first-person lyric utterance. Yet Brainard's strophic pulsations diffuse their "I" across a potentially infinite field of vernacular circumstance—schematizing this self's tangential relation to "all that is the case," and thereby calling for an expanded definition of postwar serial statement (Wittgenstein, 5).

Consequently, I have enacted my own rudimentary rounds of Barthesian Prisoner's Base: scattering critical "catechisms" concerning serial, Pop, and Language poets, so as to let their disparate-seeming projects commingle under the auspices of an art-historical discourse attuned to additive composition, to epistemic translatability and to collectivist-tending productivism. Within this context, I hope to have demonstrated that Brainard's all-over mode of making "simple" sense could stand as compelling complement to the conventional Language synthesis (localized ambiguity, followed by comprehensive theoretical supplementation), if Brainard did not operate so far in advance of postwar critical discourse that his particular type of poetic abstraction remains all but invisible.

Instead, we are left with the counterintuitive realization that a poem mapping its own myopic bondage to the solitary "I" can echo some of the twentieth century's most communally-minded ventures. Benjamin, citing Brecht, affirms that "politically it is not private thinking, but . . . the art of thinking in other people's heads that is decisive" (773). Brainard, following Whitman, elects to "celebrate" himself, to "sing" himself—confident that "What I assume you shall assume" (and vice versa). Perched between Confessionalist and Language epochs, the multifarious "I" of *I Remember* allows both for an affirmation of alienated, consumerist ego-hood, and for a revamping of prewar, utopian concord, as if the poem's latent serial statement were "We all shall remember what had seemed lost."

APPENDIX: SERIAL HISTORY

So long as Conte distinguishes serial experiments with all-over form from neo-Romantic restagings of lyric epiphany, his book provides a broad, unobjectionable framework for tracking recent installments in a postwar poetics of the "syntagmatic imagination" (98).[87] But as soon as Conte defines the serial poem as "strictly postmodern," scholarly questions arise. Poet/critic Peter Quartermain notes, for instance, *Unending Design's* failure to acknowledge the "variorum" and "indeterminate" precedent found in modernist milestones such as Pound's *Cantos* and Stein's *Stanzas in Meditation*, or to address the alternate serial-thematics present in postwar projects by Jackson Mac Low and Ronald Johnson (413).[88] For my own part, I briefly will address but two metonymic-tending projects conspicuously absent from Conte's serial pantheon (as well as from Quartermain's twentieth-century-minded supplement): the disparate-seeming corpuses of Emily Dickinson and Walt Whitman. Again, however, I do not aim petulantly to point out particular poets neglected by Conte, so much as to argue that if this critic placed poetic seriality within an expansive historical context, he would not define the postwar serial poem so constrictively.

Unending Design offers only fleeting acknowledgement of Whitman, and no reference to Dickinson—though a quick reflection upon each author's respective output confirms seriality's foundational importance to they and their postwar descendents. Considered the original introspective "mirror" and projective "window" of American poetry (in poet/critic Howard Moss's vernacular take on M.H. Abrams' "the mirror and the lamp" thesis), Dickinson and Whitman often get presented as polar opposites along a continuum mapping microcosmic (Stevensian meditation/Confessionalist monologue) and macrocosmic (Poundian appropriation/Language collage) scope in American poetry (Moss, 327). But once critics assess these august forebears as serial composers, the two poets' rhetorical strategies can be seen to overlap.

Published the year following Conte's *Unending Design*, Sharon Cameron's study *Choosing Not Choosing: Dickinson's Fascicles* (1992), for instance, long since has helped reshape canonical approaches to her subject—restoring Dickinson's excerpted lyrics to their hand-stitched place amid convoluted, "indeterminate" sequences, and thus confirming this "metonymic" poet's advocacy for "a tension previously thought . . . to reside only in the metaphoric" (Conte, 91). Strung back together by Cameron and her peers, Dickinson's closed, hermetic-seeming verses pick up the resonance of the contiguous, the aleatory.[89] Pop seriality, as Brainard's encyclopedic *I Remember* text demonstrates, offers perhaps the postwar era's most expansive response to Dickinson's centripetal stitching-together of boxed-off, episodic detail.

Along similar lines, Angus Fletcher's *A New Theory for American Poetry: Democracy, the Environment, and the Future of Imagination* (2004) revisits Walt Whitman's occasional conjecture that "the *Leaves* is only a language experiment"— recasting this poet's elastic constructions as "a harmonious ensemble of artificial and natural elements," closer to Conte's "limitless [and hence abstract] set of relations" than to Coleridge's "organic perfection of . . . outward form" (Fletcher, 290, 12; Coleridge, 53).[90] In Fletcher's account, Whitman's discrete impressions grow so manifold as to advance an all-over, "environmental" structure (a self-dispersing testimony, one that discloses the great centrifugal potential to be found even amid first-person poetic subjects) (6). Pop poetics, again, consolidates this combination of impressionistic detail and perspectival form, pushing ever further away from the fixed poetic object of New Critical scrutiny, and probing the affective realms of the writerly text. *I Remember*, I believe, evinces many of Conte's serial criteria more dynamically than do those works chosen by the critic, yet only can stand as exemplar of serial composition once seriality gets redefined beyond the parochial range of postwar, coterie-based "serial poetry."

Chapter Three

Serial Sixties: Monet, Warhol, Brainard

SERIAL EXHIBITION

In his monograph for the 1960 exhibition "Claude Monet: Seasons and Moments," MoMA-curator William Seitz describes a "'series'" (an art-historical concept still novel enough to get enclosed by quotation marks) as a set of paintings that depict "a sequential cycle of light, weather, or season" (11). In his 1968 catalogue for the Pasadena Museum's "Serial Imagery" show, curator/artist John Coplans defines a "Series" (no quotes now, but capitalized) as the product of "a single indivisible process that links the internal structure of a work to that of other works within a differentiated whole" (11).[91] Amid a decade that celebrates first Monet's additive "nature-studies," then the austere, proto-conceptualist procedures enumerated by Coplans, art prodigy Joe Brainard transforms from a precocious journal writer into a protean producer of Pop-inflected serial poems—among them the anaphora-based underground classic, *I Remember*.[92]

None of these events receives much attention in the annals of postwar poetic experiment. But by repositioning Seitz's and Coplans' texts in relation to Brainard's auto-anthological *I Remember* project (published by serial installment from 1970 to 1975), I aim to show that, however simplistic or scattered this latter work may seem, it spans the topical and structural poles of postwar serial discourse, and hence exemplifies a long-undervalued means of Pop poetic abstraction. In the hope of establishing a broad interpretive context within which best to appreciate Pop-poetry's perspectivist serial forms, I thus will outline art-history's halting steps toward embracing first Monet's serial displays, then Andy Warhol's serial compositions.

Whereas Seitz, for instance, circa 1960, still has to contend with a critical context in which Monet's most ambitious serial studies (of Rouen Cathedral, Giverny haystacks, etc.) apparently confirm this artist's premature "decline," Coplans, writing near the decade's close, not only can take for granted the paramount importance of such "full-fledged Serial macro-structures," but can use Monet's modular precedent to help secure Warhol's central place amid postwar abstract painting (Seitz, 6; Coplans, 21). Concurrently, whereas Brainard's *Selected Writings: 1962-1971* opens with a charming, miniaturistic account of the young poet's fleeting affection for Cleopatra's asp, for Henry Miller's *Tropic of Cancer*, and Cedric Gibbons' *Tarzan and His Mate*, the collection's second half contains much lengthier sequences—kaleidoscopic projects that partner encyclopedic breadth to aphoristic density. Between 1962's "Diary Aug. 4th-15th," and 1975's Full Court Press *I Remember*, Brainard's poetic development parallels post-Ab Ex art criticism's self-refining interest in serial form, as encouraged by Seitz and consolidated by Coplans.[93]

At the same time, and as I will argue here, Brainard's texts deftly negotiate some of the more contentious distinctions between Seitz's and Coplans' accounts of seriality. Whereas Seitz attributes Monet's august, "systematically cyclical" output to the artist's exhaustive assimilation of rugged nature scenes, Brainard expands the field of serial inquiry to include all the simulacral icons and shopworn affects of Cold War mass-cultural discourse (Seitz, 19).[94] Whereas Coplans' theory-heavy text occasionally draws the overstated conclusion from its axiomatic premises (example: "the viewer can only feel, as Warhol does, a great sense of pity and compassion for all human beings"), Brainard finds it sufficient to say:

> I like Andy Warhol. I like Andy Warhol. I like Andy Warhol. I like Andy Warhol. I like Andy Warhol. I like Andy Warhol. I like Andy Warhol. I like Andy Warhol. I like Andy Warhol. I like Andy Warhol. I like Andy Warhol. I like Andy Warhol. I like Andy Warhol. I like Andy Warhol. And that is why I like Andy Warhol. (Coplans, 130; Brainard, *Selected*, 20)

Here the modular processes of Pop serial painting literally inscribe themselves onto Brainard's "Andy Do It" text, an apparent homage to Warhol's 1962 "Do it Yourself" canvases. Andy Warhol may not, as Brainard's piece puts it, "do creative paintings," yet he has "creative ideas," among them an elastic sense of serial-composition's proper scope and subject—a flexibility Brainard rapidly transfers to Pop poetics ("Andy Do It" appears in 1963).[95]

Thus while the personal acquaintance and/or aesthetic kinship between Brainard and Warhol has been noted (by Reva Wolf, Ron Padgett, Lewis Warsh), this localized connection also can serve, I will argue, as the basis for a more expansive comparative-study of serial composition in Pop painting and Pop poetics. One obvious distinction between Brainard's and Warhol's careers, for instance, concerns Warhol's relatively swift commercial/critical success as serial painter, versus Brainard's continued obscurity as serial poet. And it is within this particular context that the "fluctuating estimate" (Seitz's phrase) of Monet's own serial project proves pertinent (6).

Contemporary audiences—twenty-first-century citizens used to encountering Monet reproductions on coffee mugs, umbrellas and handbags—may take for granted this painter's status as promethean precursor to postwar serial imagery.[96] To those readers already inundated by Impressionist poplars, water-lilies, haystacks, I apologize for pushing Monet-consciousness further past any desirable point of saturation. But the varying appraisals that Monet's serial studies face, following his death, combined with these projects' rehabilitation in the months preceding Pop art's emergence as a viable aesthetic practice, can provide, I believe, for fertile inquiry, for renewed reflection concerning not only Pop paintings, but also Pop poems.[97]

Whether or not poet/collagist Joe Brainard, for example, spent much time contemplating Impressionist canvases, a brief examination of William Seitz's and John Coplans' timely texts confirms Monet's importance to subsequent reconceptualizations of representational/abstract dichotomies—to critiques of the concentrated masterpiece, and valorizations of the all-over display.[98] Amid Monet's shifting status within the Impressionist/post-Impressionist, modernist/postmodernist canons can be found, I will argue, an art-historically grounded (less biographically minded) approach to serialized poetic narratives such as Brainard's. Yet art-history's erratic response to Monet's distinctive combination of iconic, quotidian scene and integrated, conceptualist design also anticipates, as I will claim, my current dilemma of how best to establish Pop-inflected New York School authors (Joe Brainard, James Schuyler, Eileen Myles, David Trinidad among them) as bona fide experimental poets. Here I briefly defer to art-historical narrative, if only to outline, by extension, the ambiguous place of a postwar Pop poetics perched between lyric and Language camps.

SERIAL INSTANTANEITY

Since the plastic, polymorphic "I" of Pop poems most often receives recognition for its purported autobiographical acuities, I begin with a roughly analogous conception of Claude Monet's proto-Pop oeuvre as an "unprejudiced" arena of perceptual "instantaneity" (Seitz, 16, 43). More specifically, I present curator William Seitz's conflicted effort to contextualize Monet's serial project amid prevailing Ab Ex paradigms as a case-study of astute critics' mid-century response to residual modernist discourse concerning authentic agency and autonomous form (the very terms by which late-twentieth-century scholars will distinguish mainstream and experimental poetry).

As the first critic to complete a book-length study of Abstract Expressionism, Seitz seems the ideal personage to publicly expound upon this epochal movement's relation to art-historical precedent.[99] Within this context, Monet's atmospheric reveries appear the perfect place to start. The Impressionist master's almost-opaque output helps to legitimate more recent "all-over" compositions, just as de Kooning's and Pollock's monumental paintings prove the prescience of Monet's most prodigious canvases.

Still Seitz, composing his monograph for the 1960 "Claude Monet: Seasons and Moments" show, faces several critical conundrums. To begin with: because Monet's serial studies adopt oft-sentimentalized iconographic tropes, and employ a quasi-mechanical means of construction in order to reproduce these figures en masse, such projects can be hard to reconcile with an Abstract Expressionist aesthetic emphasizing (in critics Clement Greenberg's and Harold Rosenberg's terms) the medium-specific, existentially grounded actions of an authentic creative agent:

> the essence of modernism lies in the use of the characteristic methods of a discipline to criticize the discipline itself . . . The limitations that constitute the medium of painting—the flat surface, the shape of the support, the properties of the pigment—came to be regarded as positive factors, and were acknowledged openly. (Greenberg, "Modernist Painting," 94)

> With traditional esthetic references discarded as irrelevant, what gives the canvas its meaning is not psychological

> data but *rôle*, the way the artist organizes his emotional and intellectual energy as if he were living in a situation. The interest lies in the kind of act taking place in the four-sided arena, a dramatic interest. (Rosenberg, "The American Action Painters," 29)[100]

Just as Pop art's readymade, repetition-friendly constructions will elide this esoteric form of organic "action" (again, both in Pop painting *and* in Pop poetry), so Monet's voluminous variations-on-a-theme might appear lacking in both the "Ab" and "Ex" categories outlined above.

More surprising, however, is a second curatorial challenge faced by Seitz—the fact that Monet's serial projects long had been considered his least significant contribution to modernist aesthetics. Along such lines, Seitz offers this striking account of why Monet's haystacks and cathedrals "lay all but forgotten" for a quarter-century following the artist's death:

> To cite but two random examples . . . the Haystack series, hailed as a revelation of 'the poetry of the universe' when it was exhibited in 1891, was commonly regarded as an unfortunate venture by the 1940s; the series representing the façade of Rouen Cathedral, described in 1895 as a "thunderous revelation of what the modern spirit can do when allied with ancient art" appeared to a world-famous critic [Kenneth Clark] in 1949 as a "disastrous" choice of subject matter because "grey Gothic facades do not sparkle." (50, 6)

The hard-edged abstractions of Cubism, Suprematism, and De Stijl (those “flat” canvases that Greenberg presumably has in mind when describing “the essence of modernism”) can make Monet’s modular, mimetic-tending panels look timid by comparison. At the same time, Monet’s own deviation from familiar illusionistic designs (his “sparkling” Gothic facades, for instance) remains unpalatable to more tepid tastes. As soon will prove problematic for Warhol’s and Brainard’s early Pop experiments, constrictive abstract/representational dichotomies hold little space for Monet’s serial-realist projects.[101]

Consequently, Seitz cannot resist the temptation to humanize (also to heroize) Monet in conformance with triumphant accounts of Ab Ex painters’ “positive” agency and “dramatic” actions. Here it becomes clear, for instance, why Seitz’s *Seasons and Moments* monograph begins by consolidating biographical depictions of Monet as an unusually robust painter—able to endure the most unwelcoming climes, and expand his perceptual appetite accordingly. Seitz in fact starts his study by (emphatically) attributing Monet’s prodigious output to this artist’s “drive to capture the full range of natural effects, however impalpable or transitory”:

> it is just this characteristic that should first be understood if one is to know Monet: *the diversity of his landscape paintings derives directly from that of nature, to which, without need for metaphysical justification, he was entirely devoted.* (8, 5; italics in original)

Images of Monet—or his children, at least—hauling canvases through any manner of rain- or snowstorm permeate Seitz's depiction of the painter's stoic "ability and strength, physical and moral" (5).

Of course, to a contemporary audience, several generations removed from macho, mid-fifties Ab Ex rhetoric (and/or disinclined toward any analogous appeal to astringent poetic authenticity), Seitz's celebration of Monet's physical prowess and upright character (of his subject's "unswerving determination to paint truthfully the world in which he lived") can sound dated (6). Yet, as I argue below, Seitz's dual emphasis upon Monet, transcriber-of-the-organic-instant, and Monet, progenitor-of-modern-serial-composition, sets the paradoxical tone later picked up by Brainard scholarship (Joe the modest miniaturist, Joe the compulsive constructor of kaleidoscopic installations). For in both cases, an artist's deliberate diffusion of fixed, testimonial vantage—dissolved through the serial presentation of discrete, modular units—gets obscured by posthumous paeans to the man "behind" the work.

Undoubtedly, something similar could be said about any number of undertheorized artists. But the comparison between Monet's postwar legacy and Brainard's personal growth takes on greater focus, given that the former's critical status changes so drastically (from burnt-out Impressionist, to proto-Conceptualist) during the latter poet/collagist's most dynamic decade of aesthetic development, and given the quick succession of 1960's "Seasons and Moments," 1961's "The Art of Assemblage," 1962's "Campbell Soup Cans," and 1968's "Serial Imagery" shows—each anticipating Brainard's readymade mode of Pop serial poetics.[102]

In subsequent pages, I will demonstrate how critics' emphases upon Brainard's (or Warhol's) eccentric character have helped to obscure structural affinities between Pop and proto-Pop serial composition (both in painting and in poetry). First, however, I feel compelled to acknowledge that Brainard (in the guise of "instantaneous" landscape poet) often courts such a cursory reading of his work, culling the moment's scattered trivialities into quasi-diaristic texts, as with "Aug. 29, 1967" from *Selected Writings*:

> I'm outside sun-bathing on Kenward Elmslie's lawn in Calais, Vermont. I would say that it's about 10 o'clock. I'm all covered with sun tan lotion. The sun is not shining. The sky is total gray clouds. You never can tell about Vermont, tho . . . I'm going to listen real close and try to hear all the sounds I can hear.------------I hear birds chirping. The water fall. Flies buzzing around.---------
>
> (*Selected*, 34).

Biographical inverse of Monet the fugitive-moment hunter, Brainard the idling Pop-lyricist rests content to absorb what comes his way, to postpone any constrictive editorial cut, to abnegate his place as decisive aesthetic-agent and revel in the role of passive witness. Even more so than his Confessionalist, Deep Image and ecologically minded contemporaries', Brainard's authentic voice here seems to derive from devotion to the instantaneous scene (the "continuous present" of a blissed-out Gertrude Stein). Posthumous paeans to sweet "Saint Joe" appear prefigured in this bath of backyard beatitude.

Yet even prostrate upon the lawn, Brainard cannot help situating himself atop a pointed art-historical trajectory:

> There is something that I lack as a painter that de Kooning and Alex Katz have. I wish I had that. I'd tell you what it was except that I don't know. I can see myself as a Cornell or a Man Ray, but somehow I doubt that I'll ever be a de Kooning or an Alex Katz. Of course, you never can tell. I work hard and I'm smart. There is a hornet buzzing around me.------------------ (35)

Recalling Emily Dickinson's fatal detection of a "fly buzz" (also James Schuyler's preemptory expulsion of a hornet from the 1966 Frank O'Hara elegy, "Buried at Springs"), Brainard's bucolic calm barely can muffle a droning preoccupation with his own place in the modernist pantheon. With this tentative assumption of Joseph Cornell- or Man Ray-status, moreover (no minor claim for a famously humble artist, still in his mid-twenties), Brainard hints at how a diffused affection for the dispensable moment might accommodate (as Cornell's collage-like boxes, and Ray's indexical prints, have done) the aesthete's demand for compositional rigor. Brainard's faux-begrudging identification with these two eclectic, avant-garde stalwarts suggests his self-conscious construction of a proto-Pop genealogy, a queer-inflected lineage (at least compared to Katz,and de Kooning) in which lying on the lawn "all covered in sun tan lotion" (and, most importantly, taking time to tell us about it) can stand in for heroic art-making and/or urgent confession. Just as, in Monet's cyclic nature-studies, each "instantaneous" brushstroke and "unmediated" canvas stubbornly insists upon its modular place within a greater sequence, so Brainard's backyard rhapsody flouts fixed conventions concerning the ecstatic lyric moment or the conclusive autobiographical testimony—proffering provisional self-evaluations in place of epiphanic insight.

"Aug. 29, 1967," might end with its author reconciled to immediate circumstance: "Ron [Padgett] just went inside with his blanket saying it is going to rain. And it is. I can feel drops already. I guess I'll go inside too" (36). But even amid this early, improvisational project (a predominantly un-indented text, punctured by long, extensional lines: "There is a tiny breakthrough in the sky---------------Now it's gone"), the distancing effects of serial display begin to graft themselves upon Brainard's seemingly open, all-inclusive vision (36). Forever afterwards, as *Selected Writings*' interstitial notations beget *I Remember*'s modular units, such testaments to the "fugitive," "tiny breakthrough" moment (indexical accounts akin to Man Ray's rayographs) will not be banished from Brainard's work, but they will get boxed off into Cornell-like cabinets-of-curiosity.[103]

SERIAL DISPLAY

Seitz's intermittently idealized account of Monet's "organic" picture cycles can obscure the formulaic, quasi-industrial processes that link such work to postwar mass-production (38).[104] At his best, however, Seitz provides a vigorous attempt to establish Monet's tenuous, transitional place upon the continuum between classic mimesis and modern abstraction. Most important within my present study of

Pop-inflected compositional practice: Seitz asserts that the ambient, all-over nature of individual Monet canvases gets intensified—perhaps first gets noticed—through a comparison of interrelated panels, through serial display. However virtuosic Monet's ability to "tender [his] impressions in the face of the most fugitive of effects," it is the moderate (modulated) contrast from one iconic canvas (one cathedral, one haystack) to the next that best evinces this painter's apprehension of that most "fugitive" aesthetic phenomenon, the "total environment" (30). Here seriality's reduction of content, its repetition of motif, prove crucial. The compulsive-seeming cropping of reality down to elemental forms (or, at least, to interchangeable parts) trains our perception upon "optical mixture [rather] than calligraphic naturalism" (19).[105] A single haystack painting appears to be about haystacks, whereas multiple haystack paintings (hung side-by-side) offer variations on the theme of "induced coloration" (19).

During the decades between Monet's death and Seitz's show, however, institutional constraints obscure this meta-compositional component to the painter's serial project. For Monet's peculiar mode of pictorial innovation—treating the individual canvas not (or not only) as a transparent window onto the mimetic scene, but as a modular panel (a single unit amid a greater serial arrangement)—depends upon a decidedly unpropitious commercial context: galleries might gather Monet's cyclic paintings for impressive aggregate display, but only so that individual works can be sold, scattered like a litter of puppies.[106] However destabilizing to bourgeois conceptions of the self-contained easel-painting, belle époque serial displays could not sustain themselves for long, given the art-market's swift revenge in the form of imperturbable salesmanship.

Only with the Cold War expansion of a consumerist economy (with the increased international coordination of blockbuster retrospectives, the enhanced quality and distribution of photographic reproductions) does this market-driven obscurity begin to reverse itself. Only at Seitz's 1960 show do critical audiences concur with Monet's contemporary, statesman Georges Clemenceau, who had written, in response to the 1895 exhibition of 20 Rouen Cathedral paintings at Paris' Durand-Ruel Gallery, that "'With twenty pictures the painter has given us the feeling that he could have . . . made fifty, one hundred, one thousand, as many as the seconds in his life'" (Seitz, 31). This sense of infinitely expansive potential, as recognized by Clemenceau, and restored by Seitz, relies upon compositional risks inherent to serial construction—to a sequence in which each separate unit appears as pertinent as any other, but also in which any one modular scene, if isolated and made to stand on its own, may seem far less compelling than the typical self-contained canvas. In subsequent sections of this chapter I argue, by analogy, that the close-reading or selective citation of Pop serial poems such as Brainard's can prove equally problematic. But first I want to continue this study of how postwar critics' rehabilitation of Monet's nature cycles can refine our conceptions of Pop serial display.

In his 1968 *Serial Imagery* monograph, critic/curator John Coplans, for example, writes eloquently regarding the site-specific constraints imposed upon painters prone to serial composition: "Only when paintings of a Series are exhibited together in a gallery space do the parameters built into the paintings and their reciprocal quality begin to operate" (15). Picking up Seitz's lead, Coplans recounts the urgency with which Georges Clemenceau pressed acquaintances to attend Monet's 1895 Durand-Ruel show.

For Coplans detects, within the elder critic's praise, an astute anticipation of art-historical aporia:

> Clemenceau was keenly aware that if the whole *Cathedral* Series was broken up by the paintings being sold separately, Monet's extraordinary discovery would go underground and might never be apparent to future generations of artists. (26)

According to Coplans' retrospective take, no matter how famous any one particular haystack or water-lily canvas might become, its greater serial context can remain obscure, especially since "Serial imagery is concerned not with the notion of masterpiece, but of process" (17). Eliding the ineffable (by now inevitable) gestures of the Abstract-Expressionist-in-communion-with-his-canvas, Coplans' serial-painter opts to construct an architectonic (gallery-based) field—a kaleidoscopic "macro-structure" in which the viewer's engagement engenders "reciprocal qualities" ("the inherent capacity of Serial structures to interact and to reinforce by juxtaposition") (18). Serial process hence demands a criticism attuned "to the largest entity," so that its coordinated intervention into any number of formal, phenomenological, institutional and epistemic discourses can be addressed simultaneously (18).[107]

SERIAL PRODUCT

Here I would like to substantiate Coplans' somewhat vague emphases on "process," by presenting a more detailed account of how criticism addressed to the "largest entity" can enhance our appreciation of the serial text (score, painting, poem, etc.). And in order to expand upon Coplans' explanation for "how each painting fits within the chosen structure," I briefly will consider critic Benjamin Buchloh's account of Andy Warhol's 1962 "Campbell Soup Cans" exhibition (at the Ferus Gallery in Los Angeles) (18). Buchloh's piece offers, I claim, a more recent art-historical analogue to Clemenceau's *fin-de-siècle* hunch concerning serial installation. For like his predecessor's prescient detection of an additive, metacompositional power, Buchloh's analysis of Warhol's "Soup Cans" show tracks the institutional critique posed (then swiftly diffused) by successful serial display. The legacy of Warhol's Ferus Gallery project provides, I will argue, explicit confirmation of how market-driven dispersal not only can obscure the medium, but can distort the message of a pictorial series.

In his 1989 essay, "Andy Warhol's One-Dimensional Art: 1956-66," Buchloh stresses the need to reconsider Warhol's initial presentation of the Campbell Soup Can paintings (subsequently disseminated through sales and reproductions) as modular parts of a comprehensive series. Along these lines, Buchloh points out that Warhol's installation of thirty-two paintings at Ferus Gallery corresponded to the thirty-two varieties of Campbell Soup available at the time—that Warhol even checked off a Campbell's Soup product-list as he completed the project. Whereas Monet, in Clemenceau's account, hints that he could have painted a canvas for every second of life, Warhol self-consciously restricts himself to "canned," prefabricated categories. Here the relationship between individual painting (standard unit of private art consumption) and complete series (alibi for latest commercial display) poses many provocative questions. Most obviously: what are we to make of a pictorial set whose parameters depend not upon internal/organic logic (the artist's impassioned resolution of a formal problem, or spontaneous sketch of the natural environment), but upon crass commercial constraint? What value will each discrete item (painting, soup can) possess once stripped from its symbolic place in the collective (and collection-minded) consumer consciousness? By displaying a line of serial products (a compendious, quasi-autistic catalogue pitched as much to the ad-man's conceptual eye as to the typical-shopper's tepid palate), Warhol's "Campbell Soup Cans" show serves not only to parody mass-cultural choice, but to critique (also to condone) the commodity-sign's swift replacement of art's empirical objecthood.[108] Ready to stand as isolated, emblematic representations of the all-over project that they comprise, Warhol's reified canvases (unlike Monet's mutually enhancing panels) beg to be taken home, and in whatever form: real or copied.

Critics long since have made the case for Warhol's Pop icons embodying an ambivalent late-capitalist critique. But Buchloh's pointed restaging of the Ferus Gallery show (of Warhol's peculiar, yet oft-overlooked attention to how "each painting fits within the chosen structure") further strengthens this scholar's claim that "the paintings' *mode of display* was as crucial as . . . their commercial readymade iconography":

> Standing on small white shelves running along the perimeter of the gallery in the way that display shelves for consumer objects would normally function in a stall,

> the paintings were still attached to the wall in the way that pictures would traditionally be installed in a gallery. (30; italics in original)

Perched upon the threshold between iconic part and abstract whole, Warhol's soup cans convoke the transcendent unity Clemenceau detects in Monet's cathedrals, even as they foreground their own position along the front lines (the "small white shelves") of market-driven dispersal. With typical Pop panache, Warhol here transforms an oft-concealed truth about serial display's self-eclipsing success into the impetus for an expansive ur-installation, a blasé shrine to commercial bastardization—anticipating Pop poets' arrangements of echoing ephemera into incremental meditations upon "everyday life."

Of course, once Warhol's Campbell cans set forth to spread their Pop gospel, the painter's gallery-based critique soon gets obscured.[109] A single, monumentalized soup can seems better-suited to calendars, postcards and t-shirts than does the 32-can ring Warhol wraps around Ferus Gallery. Subsequent audiences thus get introduced to Andy Warhol the consumer fetishist, rather than Andy Warhol the epistemically minded, proto-installationist social critic. Scholarly accounts, moreover, consolidate this myopic emphasis upon classic Warholian "content" by, in Buchloh's terms, "foregrounding discussions of Warhol's pop iconography," hence wrenching this artist's work from its "intricate reflection on the status and substance of the painterly object and . . . the definition and display of painting" (29). Warhol's deadpan examination of asymptotic difference (Vegetable, Tomato, Tomato Rice) gets lost, and his discrete panels lose their distinctive flavor—just as a lack of comparative study obscures Monet's orchestration of "total environment." Nonetheless, within the postwar context reconstructed by Buchloh, it is worth recalling that Warhol displays his numerous product-series (Brillo boxes, Coca-Cola bottles, etc.) not long after the vaunted individualists and painterly purists of Abstract Expressionism begin cranking out their own variations upon an easily recognizable, imminently reproducible theme (Robert Motherwell's Elegies to the Spanish Republic, Barnett Newman's zip-paintings, etc.), all according to the American economy's preferred model of scale: one per potential buyer. Seriality, Warhol's soup cans seem to say, will extract its own revenge on the singular masterpiece.

SERIAL PAGE

Warhol's Soup Can paintings differ from Joe Brainard's quasi-autobiographical literary projects in obvious ways. The former works reproduce an impersonal, reductive, industry-derived iconography. The latter texts depict an idiosyncratic, detail-oriented, homemade subjectivity. Yet the affinities between Pop-painting and Pop-poem quickly manifest once Pop art's rhetorical processes get surveyed—as with John Coplans' phenomenological account (in his 1970 essay, "Early Warhol: The Systematic Evolution of the Impersonal Style") of viewers' initial response to a characteristic Warhol canvas:

> The imagery that Warhol finally selects is in the range of charged, tough notions that in [Robert] Rauschenberg's

> work, for example, become transformed by painterly handling. Warhol's imagery is transformed . . . but the crucial issue is that the transformation is not immediately apparent. More immediate to the viewer is that the painting looks as disposable as the original it is modeled from: something to be thrown away, or the cheapest kind of advertising, of no value except as a message to sell. (53)

As with Rauschenberg's collage-like combines and Jasper Johns's bronze-casted beer cans, as with Allen Ginsberg's encyclopedic odes and Jack Kerouac's speech-based rhapsodies, Pop art appropriates its ostensible subject from vernacular discourse, and thereby contests the formal autonomy of postwar aesthetic objects (painting, sculpture, poem, novel). Yet Pop art also, and unlike the mid-century milestones listed above, refuses to secure a fixed place for itself *outside* of the everyday ephemera it celebrates. Whereas Rauschenberg, Johns, Ginsberg, and Kerouac foreground the deliberate "transformation" of vulgar data into exquisite art, Warhol's iconic panels and Brainard's readymade diaries often appear just as "disposable" as the originals that they get "modeled from."

Thus if Pop art picks up any cultural value beyond that of the commodity fetish, of the postcard message, it does so implicitly—by posing epistemic problems that formalist art appraisal obscures. Warhol, as Buchloh has argued, heightens viewers' awareness of the commercial context within which paintings get exhibited. Accessible affect engages his audience, yet site-specific serial installation precludes total immersion in any one canvas (leaving the turned-on consumer/spectator to windowshop a spare, 360°

display). Brainard, as I demonstrate below, likewise directs readers' attention toward convoluted rhetorical vectors, to hermeneutic tensions between (local) syntactic progress and (global) page design, between printed leaf and bounded book.[110] Though transparent as the typical image-based poem, Brainard's serialized splicings of tangential reference resist categorization as "instantaneous" records, and thus confound late-twentieth-century distinctions between abstract and realist poetry.

Most notably, perhaps, Brainard's time-tracking texts (journals, travelogues, etc.) probe poetic temporality with the conceptualist verve that Warhol brings to serial display. For just as viewers of Warhol's 1962 "Campbell Soup Cans" installation confront both thirty-two distinct flavors *and* one comprehensive product line, so readers of Brainard's diary projects encounter detached, dissociated entries *and* cohesive, composite narratives. In "Diary Aug. 4th-15th," for instance (begun, coincidentally enough, the very night that Warhol's "Soup Cans" show closes in Los Angeles, and thus offering an auspicious start to *Selected Writings, 1962-1971*), Brainard's supposedly discrete, one-a-day prose blocks read more like sculpted strophes from a carefully calibrated monologue, a camp-inflected Thomas Bernhard rant:

> *Aug. 4*—Today went to the Museum of Modern Art to see the mummified remains of the actual asp that Queen Cleopatra used to kill herself with: a most interesting object.
>
> *Aug. 5*—Today went to the Museum of Modern Art to

study Excalibur, with which King Arthur proved his right to Kingship, and to sip coffee in the Museum's sculpture garden. I found the sword to be a most unusual object.

Aug. 6—Today I thought: A rusty old sword and a dead snake? Are they kidding? Where are the real treasures of yesterday?

Aug. 7—Today I went to the Metropolitan Museum of Art to look at the *real* treasures of yesterday. Their major treasures are exciting. I found their minor treasures rather unexciting.

Aug. 8—Today I thought seriously about Excalibur and decided it could just as easily have been Prince Valiant's or even Flash Gordon's. I have definitely decided this to be a minor treasure. (12)

With date-lines running down Brainard's page (as if digits from a Jasper Johns number-painting), "Diary Aug. 4th-15th" evokes less the fugitive present of the "instantaneous" canvas than the consistent pace of the accountant's calendar—scrupulous sister to diurnal time. Still, fugue-like repetitions ("Today went . . . Today I thought . . . Today I went . . . Today I thought") convene the continuous pleasures of serial display ("a most interesting object . . . a most unusual object"), as much as they conjure the daily grind of diaristic progression. A Pop *recherche du temps perdu*, Brainard's text invites readers both to revel in the moment ("to sip coffee in the Museum's sculpture garden"), and to span across eons (to compare Excalibur to Flash Gordon's sword). However charming line-by-line, "Diary Aug. 4th-15th" demands, in Coplans' terms, analysis addressed "to the largest entity."

Again, in "Jamaica 1968," Brainard assumes the kaleidoscopic journal-keeper's convoluted pose, required to give himself up to the moment, yet equally concerned to move his plot along:

> MARCH 3rd
>
> Our house is a little house up on top of a big hill . . . We have a swimming pool and two maids. I don't like having two maids . . . There are buzzards that fly very low. And geese. They come around and drink from the pool, quack, and do enormous piles of green shit. And there are brown goats, and beautiful peacocks. I would say about a hundred of them. I have never seen anything more beautiful.
>
> MARCH 4th
>
> I'm outside sun bathing. There is a goose over by the swimming pool. Jane [Frielicher] thinks it is something else that does the green shit piles but I'm sure it's the geese . . . Beyond the bay is Montego Bay: the city . . . We really do have a terrific view up here.
>
> MARCH 5th
>
> The peacocks woke us up this morning with their various noises. They make incredibly loud sounds . . . But Joe Hazan got up and shooed them away.

MARCH 6th

The peacocks woke us up again this morning. About six o'clock. They really are beautiful tho. (*Selected*, 42-43)

Here goose-shit piles and beautiful peacocks emerge in conspicuously well-balanced proportion. Once more, Brainard seems to edit his diary as though shaping an all-over text. Neither "honest record" (along the meticulous lines of Henry Thoreau's or Dorothy Wordsworth's journals), nor fictive construct (such as Jean-Paul Sartre's *Nausea* or Doris Lessing's *The Golden Notebook*), Brainard's alternately hammy ("I have never seen anything more beautiful") and high-handed ("I don't like having two maids") account appears closer to John Ashbery's Guadalajara-dreaming "The Instruction Manual"—to have been written by a marketing director on strike. Too prosaic or pushy for conventional lyric tastes, Brainard's text can sound as "disposable" as "the cheapest kind of advertising." Yet it continues this poet's rigorous examination of the instant's relation to the durational whole, of the indented passage's position on the all-over page.

As if further to foreground this concern with serial display, Brainard begins, in subsequent projects, to insert unbroken typographical lines, perforating his situation-based poems into semi-distinct measures:

Writing
Smoking
Drinking a beer
So as to get more so

(More drunk)
To get more sleepy
(To sleep)
Listening to "The Supremes"
Almost Christmas
Almost a New Year
(*Selected*, 98)

Just as seasonal change may seem to dilate during the holiday-heavy weeks before New Year's, so "December 22, 1970" interposes mild impediments to the reader's progress— restoring attention to our temporal passage through what otherwise appears a swift, almost-instantaneous poem, plunging in vertical descent. Impromptu autobiographical reference ("Drinking a beer," "Listening to 'The Supremes'") yields to soft compositional constraint. Space and time get entangled amid Brainard's typographical scoring of the text.

By 1971's "Some Train Notes," moreover, the collagist/poet systematically deploys this conspicuous line, as if in direct homage to the small white shelves of Warhol's serial display:

Riding a train is pretty funny.
Especially when you don't really feel like you've "been" where you've been.
Especially when you don't know exactly what you are going back to or why.
Especially when you're totally stoned out of your head.
(*Selected*, 104)

Perched atop their graphic grooves, Brainard's boxy entries stand separate but combined, invoking both the college-ruled page and the schoolboy's digressive "theme." As with Warhol's Campbell soup cans, each utterance appears eminently detachable ("This train stop is a long one"; "A woman just sat down next to me"), yet loses its distinctive flavor set alone. Precursor to Barthes's *S/Z*, Brainard's strophic account accentuates the seme's (also the seam's) manifold meanings (the poet's floundering analysis of not having "'been'" where he's been, for instance, picks up comic precision once we learn that this sentiment springs from somebody stoned "out of" his head).

Fragmentary, subjectless sentences may stumble toward a camp epiphany on the passage of time:

> I can see my own face now more than I can see what's outside.
> I guess I'll stop now and try to read some Lillian Helman. (106)

But throughout the piece, Brainard's grid-like depiction of temporal/geographical progress offers abstract counterpoint to more familiar forms of modernist reverie. It is as if Walter Benjamin, enthused by the latest Mondrian exhibition, opted to systematize "Hashish in Marseilles."

Here I do not attempt to prove *Selected Writings*' poetic puissance, so much as to suggest that each project quoted above expands the parameters of Pop serial display.[111] Brainard mines the journal and one-liner forms for pocket-sized, easily transferable gems, yet nonetheless evokes the architectonic effects of Warhol's gallery installations. For as with his predecessor's "largest," context-affirming entities, Brainard's deft distributions of equivocal remarks engage our attention, even while they preclude complete engrossment in any one module. To assume, however, that this dispersion of substantive content, this diverting of lyric closure, this flaunting of accessible affect need inevitably produce an inferior text is to deny the epochal impact Pop and proto-Pop hermeneutics have had upon late-twentieth-century serial design.

SERIAL SIMULTANEITY

Incremental, yet inexorable progress through Brainard's "Some Train Notes" has deposited us squarely in the 1970s ("Being on a train is only where it's 'at' when you're on it / I *told* you I was stoned") (*Selected*, 104). But here I return to the prodigious decade (both for Brainard and his Pop contemporaries) that grants this chapter its title. I first invoke, as grandiose goodbye to fastidious early-sixties serial display ("Seasons and Moments," "Campbell Soup Cans," "Diary: Aug. 4th-15th"), Andy Warhol's mid-sixties launching of his silver mylar clouds [see Figure 5]. For the pleasures of merely circulating, as made manifest by Warhol's *Infinite Sculpture*, have much to tell us, I will argue, about Brainard's diffusive journal projects, just as the serial repetition in Warhol's silk-screens anticipate the anaphoric insistence of Brainard's *I Remember*.

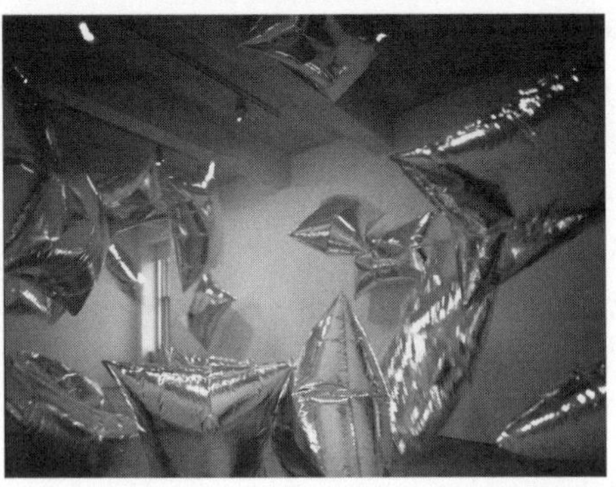

Fig. 5. Andy Warhol, *Silver Clouds [Warhol Museum Series]*, 1994
Collection of The Andy Warhol Museum, Pittsburgh

Always quick to extract revenge upon the art market's dispersive, commercially driven forces, Warhol, by decade's midpoint, appears to decide that if his architectonic installations (stacked Brillo and Heinz Tomato Ketchup boxes, etc.) must be scattered, then he himself will serve as liberator. Poet/critic Wayne Koestenbaum describes the consequent scene:

> In an audiotape that Warhol made of the unveiling of an early version of the silver clouds, on the roof of the Factory, his delight is evident, as is his conviction that ethereal objects are espoused to the sky: he squeals with joy as the silver structure (an "Infinite Sculpture") rises and disappears, blending into clouds and vacant blue. (111)

Georges Clemenceau's paean to "'the perfect equality of art and phenomena,'" as present in Monet's serial enterprise, picks up postwar resonance with the release of Warhol's buoyant sculpture (Coplans, *Serial*, 26).[112] Here, however, serial display's swift dispersal takes the form of preemptive (perhaps homeopathic) celebration. As if in accordance with the potlatch-participant's counterintuitive motives for tossing possessions off a cliff, Warhol dispatches this latest design into the "clouds and vacant blue."[113] Monet's interrelated panels may get split among myriad buyers, obscuring his picture-cycles' additive power, but shamans' logic seems to suggest that Warhol's ritualistic expenditures only can lead to bolder art-world provocations—to an endless supply of (again, Brainard's terms) "creative ideas," boomeranging back toward Warhol's roof like some Factory-kept pigeon flock.

Pushing this renunciatory/annunciatory dialectic to its extreme, Warhol claims to have abandoned painting altogether ("'I thought that the way to finish off painting . . . would be to have a painting . . . that you fill up with helium and let out of your windows'"), if only further to consolidate his art-historical pedigree: here by managing both to echo the Baudelairian dandy ("I love the clouds . . . the clouds that pass"), and to extend what Buchloh describes as a more cantankerous "Rimbaud/Duchamp tradition of self-imposed refusal of artistic production" (Buchloh, 41; Baudelaire, 1; Buchloh, 41). Casually soaring into orbit, the *Infinite Sculpture's* mirrored balloons can reflect back any number of aesthetic strategies without succumbing to argumentative heaviness. As Warhol confirms throughout his career, lightness of tone never need preclude intellectual heft.

Of course, Buchloh's biographical follow-up traces the limits to any such leisurely and/or combative posture for this workaholic, consumer-friendly artist:

> Ten years after his first declaration, Warhol (having taken up painting again) still struggles with the problem (or the pose?): "I get so tired of painting. I've been trying to give it up all the time, if we could just make a living out of movies or the newspaper business, or something. It's so boring, painting the same picture over and over." (41)

But within my present investigation of 1960s serial practice, I wish to demonstrate that Warhol's cagey pledge to scatter corpus and career need not wait for evidence from subsequent decades to prove itself disingenuous. However "indifferent," in Coplans' terms, to the number of paintings he has made, Warhol can rest assured (within months of the first Ferus Gallery show) that many of his most widely distributed serial forms will avoid being sent "underground." For such works have internalized the logic of serial display—either into the confines of a single canvas (as with the repeated silk-screens), or amid a self-declared constellation (as with the iconic panels of race riots, electric chairs, etc., that get paired to "blank" monochromes). And within this context of combinatory creation and/or coordinated repetition, it should come as no surprise that even Warhol's meandering clouds merit careful attention for what Coplans calls their serial "macro-structure."

Corralling Warhol's helium-based sculptures back into the gallery space (contra the artist's avowed desire to let his balloons "float out your window"), Coplans presents these errant clouds as yet another site-specific epistemic critique, an ever-mobile contestation to classic one-fixed-image-per-viewer paradigms:

> Perhaps no single image in the second half of the Twentieth Century is so daring in concept and so beautiful in appearance as Warhol's helium-filled Series of floating aluminum pillows . . . identical, manufactured objects remorselessly stamped out by a machine, which when filled with gas and clustered within a space, become more organic in their relationship than the interweaving strands of a Pollock painting. (*Serial*, 16)

Here Coplans' hasty, hyperbolic praise (the century's "second half" had not reached its midpoint) may echo Warhol's own ecstatic response to standing surrounded by his silver floating forms. But Coplans' corresponding conception of "macro-structure" ("each unit remains interchangeable and has the same rank as the others, without disturbing the continuity") also can prompt a detailed phenomenological account of how Warhol's dispersive pillows "interweave" their strands (11).

To begin with, Warhol's organic/manufactured clouds enable Coplans to demonstrate that even amid the most agile or elastic serial forms can be discerned a "remorselessly stamped out" procedural system:

> Central to Serial Imagery . . . is the controlling influence of the macro-structure, within which (provided the

> parameters are systematically observed) a high degree of randomness in the use of infra-forms is possible. (16)

Once made to Factory specification, and stamped with the imprimatur of art-world sophisticates, Warhol's clouds are given reign to roam where they please, extending his *Infinite Sculpture*'s compositional field into the furthest nooks of the exhibition space. Along such lines, Coplans' macro-structure concept helps to clarify this curator's ideal of criticism addressed to the "largest entity" (11). Cathedrals, soup cans and aluminum pillows, broadly dispersed across a gallery, do not depict illusionistic scenes, nor describe fixed, delineable conglomerates, but rather construct an amorphous realm of aesthetic resonance—a charged perceptual field in which the main concern (again a hermeneutic one) is how each set-piece fits within the "interweaving" structure (interweaving because, unlike more frontal paintings, Monet's and Warhol's serial installations cannot be apprehended by a single glance).

Thus however atmospheric the palette, or obvious the iconography, employed by serial display, its kaleidoscopic impact upon the viewer evokes less the Impressionistic instantaneity affirmed by Seitz, than the perspectival simultaneity described by Coplans:

> The record of Monet's eye, so to speak, betrays itself in his simultaneous views of [Rouen Cathedral's] solid, stone face; the time-spread—its sequence and duration—is compressed and magnified. Thus the normal sequence of time collapses; it becomes encapsulated by Monet's and the observer's constant shift of perception. (Coplans, 26)

Macro-structural simultaneity directs viewers' attention away from the mimetic (myopic) scene, provoking constant perceptual shifts, a compressed and magnified plurality of perspectives. Here the multiple vantages imposed by serial display preclude any unmediated image, and parallel reading's semiotic drift. Yet serial composition's "indivisible process" ("a particular inter-relationship, rigorously consistent, of structure and syntax") differs from the meta-narrative of experimental fiction, from the cumulative sweep of chronological memoir, since serial projects do not divide preexisting entities or projected wholes into constituent parts, but instead construct kinetic fields of interchangeable modules (akin to the cognitive swells concretized by Brainard's incremental prose-blocks) (Coplans, 11, 13). The converse of a characteristic Vermeer canvas, Monet's and Warhol's serial installations elicit, instead of depicting, the reading-subject—dispersing, rather than condensing, the "normal sequence of time."

SERIAL SUBJECT

Perhaps no Warholian trope better epitomizes this concern with serial "time-spread" (with a "collapse" and "encapsulation" of durational sequence) than the artist's Factory-sewn photographic sheets [see Figure 6].[114] For here lateral installment precludes dramatic arc. Whereas Eadweard Muybridge's proto-cinematic studies, for example, would seem to demand standardized, sequential viewing, Warhol's recalcitrant stitcheries threaten to jam the projector. Purported Hollywood fanatic, Warhol, in his later years, does bind together images, but according to the boxy mode of modernist serial display, rather than of film's fluid stream. However mechanized, moreover, the artist's (or his assistants') exposed needlework (in Coplans' terms, "interweaving strands") proves especially anachronistic, harkening back to the perforated plaints of Sappho's papyrus ("Sweet Mother, I the web / Can weave no more"), and Dickinson's fascicles ("And when the Film had stitched your eyes"), as much as to the celluloid reels of Warner Brothers and MGM (Sappho, 57; Dickinson, 197).

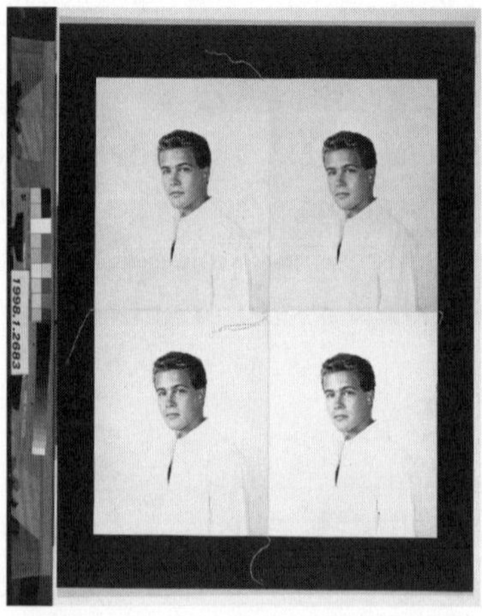

Fig. 6. Andy Warhol, *Unidentified Male*, 1986
Collection of The Andy Warhol Museum, Pittsburgh

Yet if Warhol's sewn, serial photographs thus thread together the classical lyricist's interwoven strands and the contemporary photographer's contact sheet, they also correspond, once more, to Brainard's construction of the serialized page ("Diary Aug. 4th-15th"), of the composite narrative ("Some Train Notes"). For in both Warhol's and Brainard's case, crisp, rectilinear design retains the touch of homespun tapestry, thereby affirming the historical trajectory traced by Roland Barthes (in his 1980 essay "That Old Thing Art") from ancient textile to modernist grid (with the bounded book somewhere between) (203).[115] This domesticized grid provides, in fact, perhaps art's most fitting comparison to Pop-inflected poems—an analogy I develop in previous chapters' considerations of John Elderfield's and Rosalind Krauss's essays entitled "Grids."

But here I shall close by returning to Coplans' phenomenologically minded analysis of Warhol's "floating aluminum pillow" installation, so to demonstrate that the clouds' mobile macrostructure resembles the perspectivist flux produced by *I Remember*. Constantly restitching the compositional field (with each viewer serving as roving nodal-point), Warhol's clouds trace the hermeneutic "horizon": as probed by Gadamer and Nietzsche, as invoked by Emerson's evanescent circles, and Montaigne's wraparound library-shelves.[116] Mute and impersonal as they may seem (especially in comparison to the dramatic "*rôle*" played by Rosenberg's Action Painting), Warhol's reflective clouds invite the viewer's body back into the aesthetic "arena," and thus provide a timely analogue to Brainard's affective, writerly texts.

For just as the clouds glide through a gallery space, "animated by air and viewers' body movements," so *I Remember*'s detached, breezy statements hover in Calderesque equipoise, ever-prepared to conform around a reader's perspectival proclivities:

> I remember Christmas carols. And car lots.
> I remember bunk beds.

> I remember rummage sales. Ice cream socials. White gravy. And Hopalong Cassidy.
> I remember knitted "pants" on drinking glasses.
> I remember bean bag ashtrays that would stay level on irregular surfaces. (Buchloh, 33; Brainard, 18)

Poetic equivalent of the bean bag ashtray, Brainard's malleable macro-structure constantly can recalibrate its valence in order to stay "level" with the reader's taste. Christmas carols combine with car lots—either to imply deadpan social critique, or to limn the all-inclusive range of Pop poetic retrospection. Ice-cream socials and "white" gravy confirm the vanilla-blandness of a cultural milieu defined by rummage sales and Western films, or else convoke the sturdy unpretentiousness of postwar Middle America (Warhol himself calls "a good, plain look . . . my favorite look") (68). Bunk beds and knitted "'pants'" hint at confinements and/or containments of the sexualized body, even as they suggest kid-friendly fun.[117] Taken as a whole, moreover, this passage's "compressed" sequence encourages disparate combinatory conjectures (Do horizontal car lots correspond to vertical bunk beds? Do drinking glasses with knitted "pants" complement bean bag ashtrays?). The overall meaning of any such "collapsed" and "encapsulated" (all-over) series thus depends upon the individual reader's attunement to Cold War cliché, to camp-inflected parataxis, to the "occult harmonies" Emerson celebrates in his description of philosophy's "Joyous Science" (Emerson, 567). More broadly put: *I Remember*'s "indivisible process" calls for a fused formalist/semiotic analysis—not just the magnified focus of the self-contained close-reading, but also a Barthesian catalogue of various critical vantages called forth by the kaleidoscopic text.

Before releasing Warhol's *Infinite Sculpture* from my own purview, I thus want to draw from it one final distinction, to sketch the centrifugal and/or centripetal pressures posed by serial display.[118] Launched from the Factory rooftop, Warhol's balloons scatter in a Big Bang-like spectacle (no master-frame holds these separate units together).[119] Confined within a gallery space, however, Warhol's clouds circle back and commingle, settling into sustainable oscillation, swarming then evading their audience. By analogy, Brainard's allegedly random, anti-linear text may seem to sprawl in all directions at once, yet its anaphoric repetitions track the centripetal force of a containing structure; they trace the contours of an almost-empty space (here the reader's syntactically unburdened mind), a refractive arena in which buoyant entries can bounce around, quietly reconstellating our relation to the text.[120] In both Warhol's and Brainard's projects, it is thus the centripetal strictures of serial display that allow for a sustained centrifugal "simultaneity." The small white shelves of "Campbell Soup Cans," of "Some Train Notes," emerge/recede as each artist's subsequent macro-structure encapsulates a microcosm of "seasons and moments," motion and time.

Chapter Four

Serial Realism: Poetic Narrative in Perspectives

SERIAL REALISM

For late-modernist painters opposed (in critic Clement Greenberg's terms) to "using art to conceal art," perspective-based realism proved the apex of vulgarity ("Modernist," 68). Similarly, for prominent advocates of postwar poetic experiment, the adoption of a first-person "I" limited a poem's scope to one of narcissistic confession and/or self-inflating insight. Yet this reductive preference for the abstract over the representational gets problematized with the advent of Pop—both in Pop painting, and in Pop poetics. For just as the serial repetition of Warhol's readymade icons produces as dramatic a dispersal of single-point perspective as any "flattening" of the picture-plane ever could, so Pop poetry provides as provocative a critique of Confessionalist norms as does any overtly "opaque" text (Greenberg, *Collected*, 29).

Crucial to Pop art's departure from static, single-point perspective—to its construction of a dynamic, multiplicitous perspectivism—is its reintroduction of narrative trope within the avowedly anti-narrative discourses of postwar painting and, later, poetry. Crucial to the establishment of a critical vocabulary with which better to analyze Pop poetics is an importation of the keenest conceptual apparati concerning Pop painting. Since poet Joe Brainard considered himself primarily a visual artist (an artist more comfortable, as previous chapters have noted, with the readymade materials of the assemblagist than with the neo-classical-painter's palette to which he aspired), Brainard can serve as propitious focal-point for further comparisons between these fields. In what follows, I thus want to demonstrate (using scholar Wendy Steiner's study of the convoluted relationship between perspective-based realism, and realist narrative's repeated subject, as my model) how Brainard's Pop-inflected, serial-realist corpus fuses tendencies toward epiphanic insight, imagistic mimesis, disjunctive collage and matte all-overness—all within the guise of accessible, first-person narrative.

SERIAL PERSPECTIVE

Half a millennium before Warhol's and Brainard's birth, Renaissance treatises concerning single-point perspective (here recounted by Steiner) proscribe narrative progress, even as they establish the proto-photographic template for all subsequent conventions regarding "realist" representation:

> The logic of the Albertian model, in which a picture was to represent the view of a perceiver at a fixed distance

> from the scene viewed, demanded that the perception be atemporal, a single moment of vision. (144)

Like the ecstatic lyric moment, the perspective-based image claims to offer a crystallization of acute perception—amid the eclipse of story.[121] In Leonardo's *Annunciation*, for instance, the painter constructs Gabriel's angel wings (according to popular legend) by copying from a live bird in flight, and thus conflates the sacred, hypersonic message with the artist's singular "moment of vision" [see Figure 7]. In *The School of Athens*, Raphael convokes several centuries of philosophers amid a single, spectacular assembly, thereby suggesting that the most privileged pictorial instant remains an "atemporal" one [see Figure 8]. Exemplars of Renaissance single-point perspective, Leonardo's and Raphael's paintings collapse complex narratives into dynamically constructed *tableaux vivants*.[122] "Fixed," focalized distance precludes the possibility for durational drift.

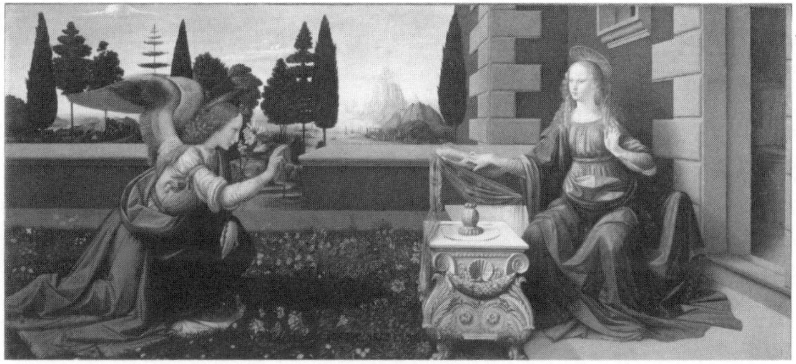

Fig. 7. Leonardo, *Annunciation*. 1472-1475

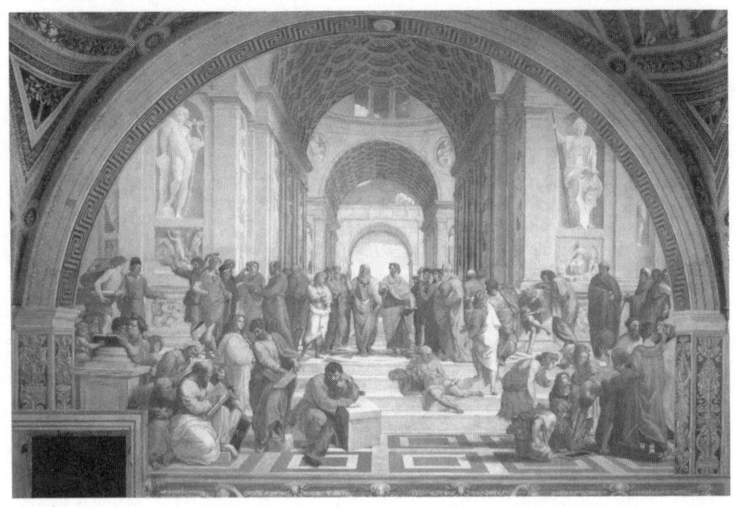

Fig. 8. Raphael, *The School of Athens.* 1510-1511

To restate this principle in terms borrowed from twentieth-century poetic criticism: the detached instantaneity of Imagist description ("Petals on a wet, black bough"), the tortuous simultaneity of Confessionalist retrospection ("One dark night . . . I watched for love-cars . . . My mind's not right") can appear impossible to reconcile, even within a project that equally depends upon swift, impressionistic notation and sweeping cumulative affect (Pound 251, Lowell 190). A century after Poe's categorical pronouncement, the long poem remains "a contradiction in terms," and one obvious way to evade this contradiction is to shun narrative construction and/or psychological reflection altogether (Poe 71). Within this context, the obliteration of perspective through anti-referential writing certainly can seem a more legitimate means of poetic innovation than do the incessant additions of anecdotal fact to be found in Brainard's *I Remember*:

> I remember when I went to a "come as your favorite person party" as Marilyn Monroe. (2)
>
> I remember playing "doctor" in the closet. (5)
>
> I remember "The Tennessee Waltz." (6)
>
> I remember Bickford's. (7)

Yet I want to suggest several final limitations to the conventional reading of Brainard's text as a simple, straightforward autobiographical statement. Following Steiner's lead, I want to track those processes whereby the serial-realist subject and/or the incrementalist narrative (in Warhol's repeated silk-screens, in Brainard's aphoristic assertions) can prove as apt a site of abstraction as does any "deauthored" pictorial or poetic text.

SERIAL TIME

In her book-length study *Pictures of Romance: Form against Context in Painting and Literature*, Steiner traces a lively exchange between single-point perspective and "simultaneous" narrative, from fifteenth-century aesthetic treatises by Alberti and Leonardo to serial compositions by Warhol and his Pop contemporary Roy Lichtenstein (an exchange, I will argue, with much to offer any subsequent discussion of the elastic "I" deployed in *I Remember*) (Steiner, 37). To begin with, *Pictures of Romance* sketches two basic criteria by which to confirm the presence of "strong pictorial narrative": "the most important are: that the painting present more than one temporal moment; and that a subject be embedded in at least a minimally realistic setting" (2). Narrative provides a plausible progression from one moment to the next. And this durational nature of narrative would appear unremarkably obvious, were it not the case that Renaissance conventions prescribe the presentation of a *single* moment of vision, forbidding the depiction of more than one moment in time ("Nothing could be more foreign to Renaissance realism than the juxtaposition of temporally distinct events within a single visual field") (23). Like photographs, like Imagist or epiphanic poems, perspective-based pictorial compositions promise the instantaneous apprehension of a scene—unmediated or, at most, mediated through the crystalline gaze of an objective, ahistorical viewing-subject. Scholars of postwar poetic experiment easily can anticipate the insidious consequences connected to this rhetoric of timeless transparency: historically conditioned representational conventions themselves get obscured. Florentine painting's swift institutionalization of Filippo Brunelleschi's mirror-based architectural sketches seems to imply that no roving method of realist depiction is possible.[123]

But as an example of the pictorial potential concealed by dogmatic devotion to single-point perspective, Steiner considers *The Meeting of St. Anthony and St. Paul* (about 1440, variously attributed to Sassetta and the Master of Osservanza), an early-Renaissance work that charts the Egyptian saint's progress from pride, to temptation, to humility, repeating a recognizable figure winding down the lengthy desert road to redemption. Crucial to Steiner's argument is that *Meeting*'s Anthony appears in several places at once, thus precluding our apprehension of any fixed, unified scene [see Figure 9]. In its fusion of a "minimally realistic setting" *and* of multiple, temporally distinct episodes, *Meeting* conveys its impact by allowing the viewer to place Anthony's trials upon an inferred narrative trajectory—to see a coherent story in which the saint's repeated presence proves logical.

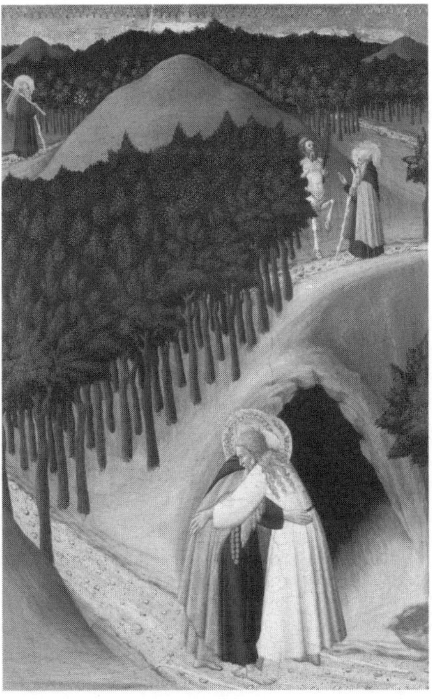

Fig. 9. Master of the Osservanza (Sano di Pierto?)
The Meeting of Saint Anthony and Saint Paul, c. 1430/1435
tempera on panel
Samuel H. Kress Collection
Image courtesy of the National Gallery of Art, Washington

By contrast, post-Renaissance "History Painting" must instruct through instantaneous illumination, rather than through any diffusive catalogue of discrete moments. Much of Steiner's study concerns the elaborate contortions to which Renaissance and post-Renaissance painters subject the picture-plane in an effort to bridge this gap between perspective-based instantaneity and narrative-based simultaneity. Brainard's poetic construction of serial time ("I remember when hoop skirts had a miniature revival. / I remember waking up somewhere once and there was a horse staring me in the face. / I remember sitting on top of a horse and how high it was") picks up, I will argue, on that pictorial precedent (22).

SERIAL STORY

Crucial to my present inquiry is Steiner's astute placement of Pop art (Warhol's silk-screen portraits, Lichtenstein's confoundings of comic-book sequence) among the first movements to depart from post-Renaissance pictorial constraint [see Figures 10 and 11].[124] And most important to Pop pictorial sensibility (at least along the art-historical trajectory traced by Steiner), is the serial repetition that distinguishes this aesthetic from a collagist mode culled by Cubism and Dada:

> It is easy to imagine . . . a triptych, for example, in which one panel shows a child laughing, another a king fighting, and a third an animal eating. Each scene is discrete, each specific, and each an action, but they lack the most

> fundamental feature of all narratives—cohesion, and, in particular, the continuity of a repeated subject. (17)[125]

Whereas the collagist (like the triptych painter imagined above) solders disjunctive iconography into a heterogeneous ensemble, the serial artist (like *Meeting*, like Warhol) brings together separate instances of the same. Whereas collage connotes an eclectic assortment of materials combined into one composite artifact, Pop serial composition suggests a homogeneity of content, a uniformity of distribution, a simultaneity of display.

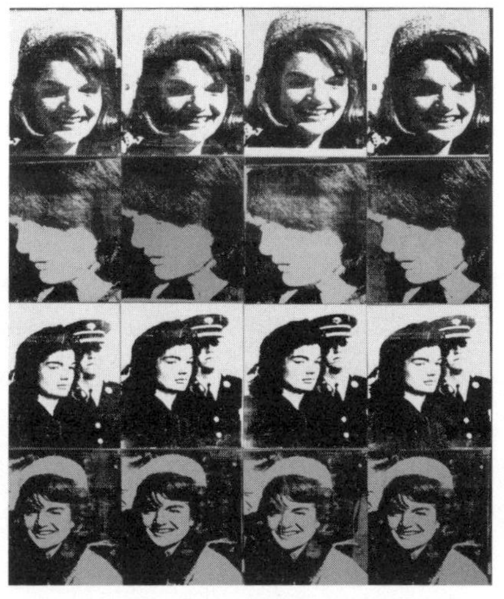

Fig. 10. 1968.2
Andy Warhol
Sixteen Jackies
1964
acrylic, enamel on canvas
$80^{3/8}$ x $64^{3/8}$”, $81^{7/16}$ x $65^{5/16}$ x $2^{1/8}$” installed
Collection Walker Art Center, Minneapolis
Art Center Acquisition Fund, 1968

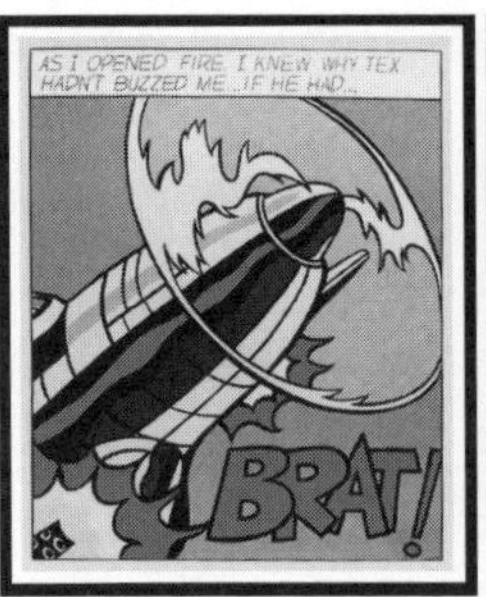

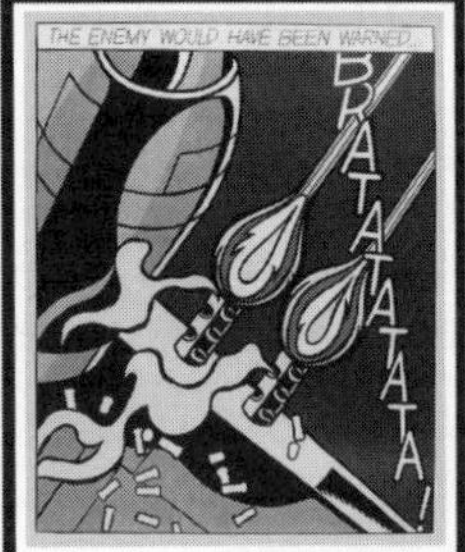

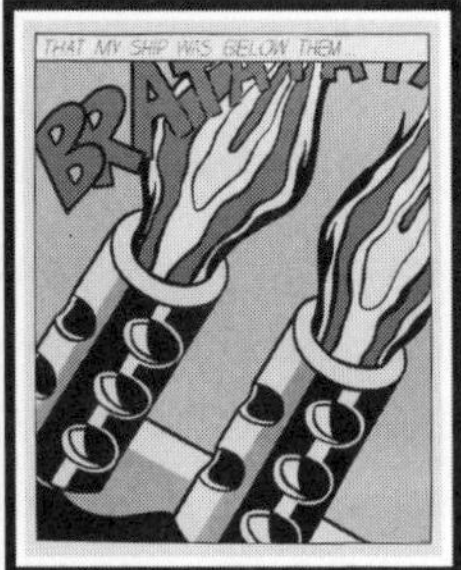

Fig. 11. Roy Lichtenstein, *As I Opened Fire Poster*, 1966

Paradoxically, this insistent presentation of the similar, this indifference to more dynamic juxtaposition, nonetheless can provide even the most anti-developmental series with an air of narrative progress. Serial narrative need not possess the conventional trappings of a compelling plot since, as Steiner argues: "the repetition of figures in a realistic rendering has the power to suggest narrative even when the events shown are not specific" (22). A postmodern *Meeting of St. Anthony and St. Paul*, Lichtenstein's *As I Opened Fire* constructs its narrative continuity, for example, not by presenting a logical, linear sequence (only in the far-right panel do we learn that the middle-panel's airplane, depicted from below, might not be that of "I" but of "I's" enemy), but by offering a consistent, if consistently modified, pictorial-subject—a repeated trope (though, again, in Lichtenstein's ambiguous construction, we cannot be certain that any two panels depict the same jet) around which the painting's discrete units cohere, even as this figure's multiple appearances preclude any potential for the single-point perspective typically associated with photographic instantaneity and, thus, realism.[126]

In the narcissistic, mirror-staged mesh of mass-media representation, moreover, Pop's emphasis upon the "repeated subject" acquires added nuance, since each varied instance of Jackie, Marilyn, or Liz suggests both a slightly modified pictorial-subject (the star in her enumerative dayglow hues), *and* a slightly modified artistic- and audience-subject (the painter presenting, the viewer projecting onto that star from a stable, if ever-shifting vantage).[127] Needless to say, these dualistic definitions of the serial subject only get further dramatized when that subject is an autobiographical one: as occasionally with Warhol and almost always with Brainard (though Brainard, astutely enough, sometimes chooses the great Andy Warhol as his poetic subject).

Along such lines, Steiner affirms Pop's fusion of serial complexity and simplistic "content," treating the movement's adoption of vulgar, vernacular motif as proof of its prioritization on epistemic intervention over virtuosic technique, or expressive statement. Here *Pictures of Romance* provides a compelling case for how Pop's systematic appropriation of consumerist icons can progress beyond the merely parodic—toward a reconfiguration of pictorial/perceptual possibility. Warhol's celebrity portraits, and Lichtenstein's asyntactic battle-scenes, pick up added art-historical nuance given their reinsertion of the repeated subject in its various guises (Jackie: fighter pilot; silk-screen painter: cartoon illustrator; star-struck spectator: comic-book reader), and their restoration of temporal (if not always linear) code to painting.

Here also, by extension, an oft-celebrated collagist line of twentieth-century American poetry (Pound, Olson, much of what typically gets classified as serial poetics, and, via Marjorie Perloff's prescient expansion of "the Pound tradition," Language) finds its obscured, undervalued complement in serial-realist texts such as Brainard's *I Remember*—projects that do not simply shore up fragments, but that artfully construct incremental narratives:

> I remember daydreams of saving someone from drowning and being a hero.
> I remember daydreams of going blind and how sorry everyone would feel for me.
> I remember daydreams of being a girl and of the beautiful toenails I would have.
> I remember daydreams of leaving home and getting a job and an apartment of my own. (78)

Placed side-by-side, Brainard's disparate daydreams (of macho heroism, glamorous self-ornamentation, and proletarian self-sufficiency) prove as climactic as does any decisive action taken on the typical protagonist's part; for, once combined, these divergent variations-on-a-theme convoke narrative cohesion.

Pictures of Romance (here borrowing from theorist Seymour Chatman) points toward this crucial counter to the serial-realist text's potential matte sprawl:

> A salient property of narrative is double time structuring. That is, all narratives, in whatever medium, combine

> the time sequence of plot events, the time of the *histoire* ("story-time") with the time presentation of those events in the text, which we call "discourse-time." What is fundamental to narrative, regardless of medium, is that these two time orders are independent. (Chatman; as quoted in Steiner, 14)[128]

Chatman's conception of "discourse-time" suggests why Brainard's perpetual interruption of story need not rob *I Remember* of narrative status. In fact, few works foreground their "dual time" structure more explicitly and extensively than does Brainard's text (Steiner 14).[129] For it is the insistent, anaphoric arrangement (quasi-autistic analogue to the discourse time constructed by Chatman's performative narrator) of kaleidoscopic reminiscence (the serendipitous "story-time" of the inspired, omnivorous memoirist) which distinguishes Brainard's Pop-inflected project from appropriative poems that, again in critic Joseph Conte's terms, reflect cultural/political/technological developments "in an unmediated way" (Conte, 17). However scattered-seeming Brainard's all-over sequence, each entry stands in direct relation to the first-person subject at his poem's propulsive center. However discontinuous Brainard's individual entries, each "I Remember" phrase confirms the continuous present (continuous pleasures) of retrospection (what image better dramatizes narrative's "dual time" structuring than that of Brainard lying down—as he tells interviewer Tim Dlugos—to tan and to draft hundreds of *I Remember* episodes?). Narrative, especially Pop narrative, demands the frequent recurrence of a familiar subject, yet narrative's reliance upon a diachronic realism necessitates that this so-called repeated subject change continuously to fit the shifting circumstances in which it finds itself. Here again, *I Remember*'s construction of a reflective/refractive narrative "I" (anathema to most contemporaneous poetic experiment) proves prescient.

SERIAL IDENTITY

Thus with Brainard's diffusive "I" in mind, and through the art-historical analogy provided by Pop's radical reconfiguration of pictorial perspective, I want to offer several partial, provisional reconceptualizations of the postwar poetic subject. For most pertinent to my present inquiry is the comparative vantage that Steiner's analysis of single-point perspective opens upon poetic criticism (specifically studies concerning the lyric moment's resilience amid a modernist era otherwise inclined to austere, all-over form). By juxtaposing Steiner's account of the "fixed" perspective's preeminence in post-Renaissance painting, and contemporaneous critiques of the "timeless" lyric's analogous place in post-Romantic verse, I hope to have suggested that a twentieth-century poetics dependent upon Imagist veracity and/or epiphanic insight offers a static scene comparable to that constructed through single-point pictorial perspective; that, like early abstract painting, Language writing offers (now as postmodern antidote to the transparent poetic subject) "the unpicturable"; and that serial-realist texts, such as *I Remember*, struggle to reconcile inclinations toward either tendency, especially as brought about by mass-cultural production.

Steiner's study can help to contextualize Brainard's Pop poetics along a continuum, for example—to begin amid the most incontestably "representational" modes of twentieth-century poetic discourse—between the impersonal, show-don't-tell Imagism of an early W.C. Williams ("munching a plum on/ the street a paper bag/ of them in her hand"), and the self-centering Confessionalism of a W.D. Snodgrass ("I tugged your hand, once, when I hated / Things less: a mere game dislocated / The radius of your wrist"):

> By prohibiting repeated subjects, painting could depict identity as either a single frozen moment or an eternal essence, but not as a continuity constantly modified by time. Thus the Renaissance system reinforced the distinction between the isolated or transcendent self and the self modified by circumstance. (Williams, 383; Snodgrass, 34; Steiner, 2)

Elliptical efforts to describe (without disturbing) the universe, and purgative attempts to assemble an idea-of-order out of acute personal experience, prove equally constrictive to the poetic subject that seeks to construct a "continuity constantly modified by time" (I remember waking up . . . and there was a horse staring me in the face. / I remember sitting on top of a horse and how high it was"). Contrasted to Brainard's paratactic pivots, Williams' clipped precision, and Snodgrass' confessional pathos can seem to exemplify the poles of post-Romantic (single-point) perspective: of perennial tensions between objective design and reflective narrative, between the contingent and the timeless lyric. Such binary schemes (analogous to Renaissance distinctions of "the self modified by circumstance," and the "transcendent self") reinforce the presumption that testimonial composition can accomplish nothing betwixt either extremity of poetic witness.

But within this context, serial-realist projects such as *I Remember* radically reconfigure the first-person "I"—now vacated of the detached impassivity or reductive universality of typical "transparent" verse, and the self-monumentalizing exhibitionism of Confessionalist poetics. Conflating and refining such oppositional-seeming tendencies, Brainard discovers the "eternal essence" of serial-identity within a sequence of discontinuous ("single frozen") moments. *I Remember*'s cyclic structure "isolates" the self, if only to amplify its status as that which gets "modified by circumstance."

Again, even upon the broader axis of representational content/experimental form, polarizing distinctions between "mainstream" (testimonial) and "avant-garde" (abstract) poetics offer evidence of a rigid classificatory split analogous to those described above: dividing lyric from Language, authenticity from artifice, mimetic imagery from diffused opacity, etc.[130] Yet Brainard's serial-realist projects (and, I should add, James Schuyler's *Morning of the Poem*, Eileen Myles's *Chelsea Girls*, Lewis Warsh's *The Origin of the World*, David Trinidad's *Plasticville*) confound any such constrictive schema by grafting amiable, quasi-autobiographical poetic personae onto spare exoskeletal structures. To be brief: just as, in Steiner's memorable summation, "It is not the medium of painting but its conventions that have reduced narrativity to an apparently peripheral concern for art historians," so it is not Language's definitive deconstructions of first-person narrative, but critics' wholesale valorizations of such attempts, that have rendered the propulsive "I" a peripheral concern for progressive poetic scholarship (9).

Moreover, though serial-realist texts such as *I Remember* might be narrative-based, this need not leave them uncritical of narrative convention. Just as "language" remains of essential importance to those who willfully interrupt standard syntax, "narrative" serves as focal point for those who complicate its seamless, all-too-easily consumable flow. Just as Language poems critique the perfunctory operations of a banalized public discourse, so Brainard's serial-realist project emerges as contemporaneous alternative to the three-minute pop song, the thirty-minute sitcom (serial compositions of a different sort, those that encourage a myopic focus on story-line, rather than on complex perspectivist construction). Yet whereas Language advocates tend to eliminate the affective-subject as a worthy component of poetic experiment, Brainard (like Warhol with his photomat strip of self-portraits, like Whitman with his self-contained multitudes) does not dismiss the first-person-confessional pose, so much as he reproduces this figure countless times—until his works' predominant performative motif becomes such perspectivally charged repetition itself.

SERIAL TESTIMONY

Along similar art-literary-historical lines, Steiner's analysis of Pop's repeated pictorial-subject can help to situate Brainard's (or Schuyler's, Myles's, Warsh's, Trinidad's) poetic corpus in relation to serial-realist texts by Gertrude Stein and John Cage. For far from abandoning the propulsive "I" (the testimonial narrative), Stein and Cage, in many of their most uncategorizable works, rely on both as much as Whitman did (given Language's paradigmatic critique of affective literary subjecthood, the chatty, campy, ventriloquistic *Autobiography of Alice B. Toklas* and *Indeterminacy* now appear much more difficult to place than do those monuments to anti-mimetic austerity: *Stanzas in Meditation* and *I-VI*). Within this context, it is not enough to acknowledge that the two latter, legendarily opaque poets occasionally adopt an accessible "I" as mere respite—for themselves, for their audience—from "serious" formal experiment. Nor does the logic of collage adequately account for projects in which short, dispersive units (Stein's displaced digressions, Cage's sixty-second stories) manage to cohere around a "continuity constantly modified by time," a continuity premised upon the quasi-autobiographical narrator. Here again, comparisons to the serialized pictorial-subject best illustrate how both Stein and Cage deploy their ubiquitous "I's"—so to inaugurate a sweeping, epistemic-minded inquiry concerning modular forms, perspectivist structure and narrative simultaneity.

Brainard's ensuing example consolidates this collective enterprise. For within the postwar era, the "repeated subject" (one that tirelessly traverses Whitman's "Song of Myself," that imperiously punctuates Stein's public lectures) gets progressively foregrounded: first by Cage's anecdotal entries, then by Brainard's anaphoric text. Anticipating poststructuralist calls to deauthor poetic production, Brainard elects not to explode or erase the "I," but (all the more devastatingly, as Warhol and Lichtenstein prove through their departures from previous abstract painting) to repeat it—confounding, rather than parodying, the lyric subject's authentic coordinates at a particular time and place.

Thus by evading classic autobiographical constraints, even as he reinforces the connection between author and "I," Brainard expands our conception of first-person realism. In comparison to most testimonial texts, *I Remember* offers something far more "real" (eschewing extravagant claim and/or taut plot development in favor of the casual anecdote, the punctum-inducing detail), and far less "realistic" (dispersing the Aristotelian unities). Brainard's project at first appears to provide a fixed focal-point of projective identification, but finally presents an amorphous, polytemporal subject beyond the range of even the most empathic reader. However endearing or adroit his mimetic capacities, Brainard (again like his Pop contemporaries Lichtenstein and Warhol) ultimately offers an incommunicable (at least according to Renaissance paradigm) scene of serialized simultaneity—bursting beyond the postcard frames of single-point perspective.

SERIAL STRUCTURE

As I have argued throughout this book (in treatments of poetic texts by artists Joseph Albers, John Cage, Claes Oldenburg, Ad Reinhardt, Joe Brainard, etc.), the affinity among abstract painting, aleatory performance, Pop silk-screen and serial-realist poetic experiment can be traced through a literal transference of modular compositional unit: from canvas, to manifesto, to time-bound story, to "I remember" entry. Part digressive litany, part lavish mosaic, each such serial enterprise addresses that basic hermeneutic question of how a work might best accentuate the discrete charms of its incremental instances, while consolidating the collective impact of the compositional whole.

Given this concern with ratio, proportion, volume, one final art-historical analogy for these projects is an architectural one, and Steiner again offers the perfect model in her examination of early, ambivalent responses to Renaissance proscriptions against simultaneous pictorial narrative:

> If one were to adopt this [perspective-based] realism with its requirement of spatial coherence, how could one indicate the discreteness of the separate events composing the narrative? It is at this point that the multi-compartmented building becomes so important as a structuring device for narrative. (37)

As in Benozzo Gozzoli's *The Dance of Salome and Beheading of St. John the Baptist* (1461-62), for example (a single painting that shows St. John about to be executed in one room, Salome dancing for Herod in another, and Salome presenting Herodias with John's head in a third), the depiction of complex interior spaces allows painters to combine any number of causally linked (hence temporarily distinct) scenes amid a structured simultaneity [see Figure 12].[131] Just as the modular "line" of modern abstract painting later manifests in the anaphoric phrase of Albers, Oldenburg, Brainard, so Benozzo's incestuous plot finds its pictorial equivalent in the Romanesque archways and ornate alcoves of Herod's palace. Precursor to the Baroque, Herod's hall of triangulated multiplicities hints that exhaustive repetition *is* expressive representation—albeit of an algorithmic sort—as much in Benozzo's *Dance*, as in Brainard's *I Remember*.

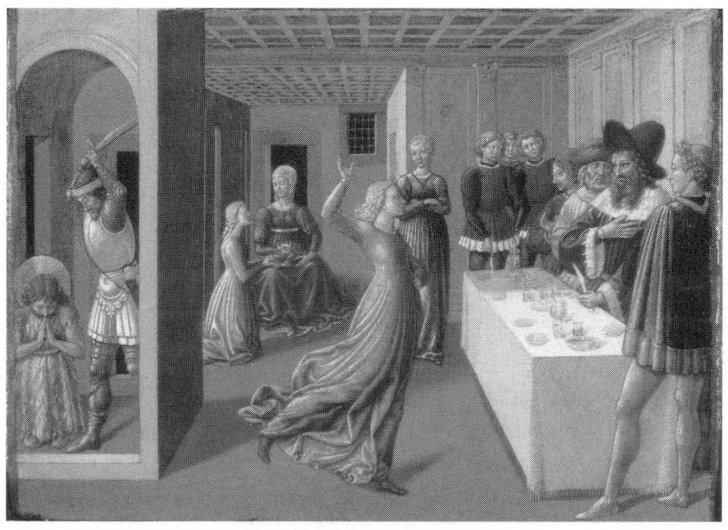

Fig. 12. Benozzo Gozzoli
The Feast of Herod and the Beheading of Saint John the Baptist, 1461–62
tempera (?) on panel
Samuel H. Kress Collection
Image courtesty of National Gallery of Art, Washington

Images of hive-like architectural space thus can serve as transitional forms along Steiner's art-historical trajectory, preserving some sense of dramatic progress within what appears a static scene:

> The building . . . changes a narrative into simultaneity, makes temporal order problematic, and thus serves as the

> natural transition of the purging of temporal flow from painting altogether. (38)

Yet even this "purging of temporal flow" often will read more as the repression, rather than the successful elimination, of narrative elements in post-Renaissance painting (modernist abstraction included, as Rosalind Krauss's analysis of the grid's conflicted purpose makes plain).[132] This latter history remains to be articulated by subsequent art-poetry comparisons. But from the present vantage it seems clear that the serial-realist text's marginal status (at least among experiment-minded critics) suggests something of an analogous, progressive/repressive transition from neo-Romantic, mid-twentieth-century verse to Language poetics, from "organic" expression to opaque "artifice"—an evacuation of sentimentality never quite complete, resulting in exaggerated hostility towards the epiphanic lyric, and in tacit silence towards ambitious experimental projects that do not deign to reinforce such reductive distinctions (Cage's *Indeterminacy*, Brainard's *I Remember*, Schuyler's *Morning of the Poem*, etc.).[133]

Steiner's *Pictures of Romance* does an admirable job confirming that the architectural metaphor retains as immediate an application in literary as in pictorial studies: reminding us that "The word 'stanza,' of course, means room"; expounding upon the "long and impressive currency" of "the conception of narrative as a procession through the rooms of a building"; citing, in particular, Spenser's analogy between "the quest and the progress through the rooms of a house," and Keats's statement, in an 1818 letter to John Reynolds, that "I compare human life to a large mansion of many apartments" (37, 193). But twentieth-century analogues to Steiner's building/poem comparison also abound.

Here I cite simply the most apropos—Joe Brainard recalling a recent nocturnal reverie:

> The other night, in bed, I was thinking about nothing in particular and I decided to try to visualize how complicated and intricate the world really is. Like every now and then, when you see a big modern apartment building, and you get a sudden flash of all that is going on inside the building. All the little rooms and all the many little people each with lots of thoughts going through each of their heads. (*Selected*, 52)[134]

If the individual life, in the age of *Endymion*, can be compared to "a large mansion of many apartments," then the aggregate Pop perspectivist-subject can be modeled on a denuded skyscraper with "all the little rooms and all the many little people." Again, it is serial-realism's emphasis upon collectivist repetition (not just collagist juxtaposition) that distinguishes its compositional logic from Language's motley mix of "Homonyms, puns, nonsense words, coinages, archaisms, learned allusions, advertising jargon" (Perloff, *Dance* 156). While language-based writing seeks to purge poetry of testimonial cliché, Brainard's paean to plain-spoken perspectivism packs in as many "little people" as possible (all named "I").

SERIAL MIGRATION

By extension, Brainard's compartmentalized entries consistently announce their own ideals of architectural order:

> I remember (here's a real let-down for you) fantasies of opening up an antique store, with only *very* selective objects, displayed sparsely in an "art gallery" sort of way.
>
> I remember fantasies of opening up an art gallery on the Lower East side in a store (I'd live in back) with one exposed wall (brick) and everything else white. Lots of potted plants. And paintings by, you guessed it, me.
>
> I remember building unusual houses in my head. One, very modern and "organic," was inside a cave. Another was mostly glass. And they all had giant bathrooms with giant bathtubs. (96–97)

Mortared together, such sparse rooms and houses (in Steiner's terms, "discrete simultaneous units") stand in for moods, for modules, the manifold chambers of which *I Remember*'s kaleidoscopic compound gets comprised (37).[135] Taken as an associative triptych, this three-part sequence illustrates, for example, how Brainard builds his eclectic edifice one entry on top of the other. Yet Brainard's book, as a whole, also exudes an "'art gallery' sort of" austerity (a spare, uniform display), with each "antique" entry offering but one "exposed wall"—one tangential edge of intimate, tactile experience. Amid its airy autonomy from plot entanglement, *I Remember*'s integral pacing proves (likes giant bathtubs in giant bathrooms) especially commodious.

For all of these reasons, I believe that *I Remember*'s retrospective honeycomb serves as multipurpose transitional form to late-twentieth-century poetics: a mausoleum for the lyric "I"; a bustling marketplace for the omnivorous bourgeois reader; an aphoristic Factory for the protean Pop subject. A Robert Moses of the post-Confessionalist age, Brainard—like William Carlos Williams in his *Paterson* persona—carries within his head not just "unusual houses," not just iconoclastic anti-lyrics, but more expansive master plans:

> I remember eating tunnels and cities out of watermelon. (35)

Contemporary to George Oppen's "world of stoops," Brainard's orally engineered watermelon provides yet another transitional template for the heterogeneous Language text soon to follow: the poem as city.

Of course, Brainard's encyclopedic range extends to the rural ("I remember the outhouse and a Sears and Roebuck catalog to wipe off with") and domestic ("I remember cold sheets in the winter time") spheres of existence as much as to the urban, the public (15, 95). Just as the numbered statements of modernist manifestos, the rhythmic scoring of John Cage's poetic projects and the repeated "I am for an art" phrases of Claes Oldenburg's anaphoric script suggest the literal trace of serial composition migrating from the painterly canvas to the writerly text, so Brainard's modular entries evoke, as poet/critic Bruce Hainley puts it, the seriality to be found "even closer at home—in books, turning a page and finding another page, the same and yet so different" (1).

Embodied within his book's discrete pages (as St. Anthony appears incarnate, yet divided among the incremental episodes of *Meeting*'s panel), Brainard's all-affirming, ultra-accessible "I" proves as omnipresent (but also as elusive) as Edmond Jabès' interrogative poetic-subject:

> To figure in the book of questions, to be part of it . . .
> To be able to say: "I am in the book. The book is my world, my country,
> and my riddle. The book is my breath and my rest."
> I get up with the page that is turned. I lie down with the page put down.
> To be able to reply: "I belong to the race of words, which homes are built with"—when I know full well that this answer is still another question, that this home is constantly threatened. (Jabès, qtd. in Caws, 679)

For all its affinity to the charming poet Joe Brainard, the "I" of *I Remember* belongs to Jabès' curious "race of words." Ever the prodigal son, the wandering Jew, this "I" consistently returns to rehabilitate what it has provisionally assembled (the "constantly threatened" home of Pop perspectivist consciousness), only to get cast out once more by the propulsive flow of serial repetition (and of poetry in the Whitmanian vein: "Till the gossamer thread you fling catch somewhere, O my soul") (Whitman, 565). Like his bardic nineteenth-century predecessor, like Jabès' "figure in the book," Brainard presents himself coming and going, constantly turning the verse line itself, even as he points toward "still another question" concerning poetry's relation to the serial painting, the serial score. Such itinerant interdisciplinarity demands the same of any criticism that would attempt to track it. Within this revisionary context, I hope to have positioned a long neglected line of serial-realist poetics somewhere between the Pop silk-screen and the contemporary Language poem—at the center (of course, as in Jabès' kabbalistic schemes, there are many centers) of postwar aesthetic innovation.

NOTES

1 As I will argue throughout this study, the periphrealization of Brainard's literary output takes two predominant forms: a critical silence regarding the poet's achievement (a not-so-benign neglect difficult, alas, to cite and to critique), and an enthusiastic endorsement of the poet's supposedly simple, modest oeuvre.

2 Brainard's 1975 Full Court Press *I Remember* offers a slightly revised synthesis of three Angel Hair Press publications: *I Remember* (1970), *I Remember More* (1972), and *More I Remember More* (1975).

3 Here Marjorie Perloff's definition of literary defamiliarization as "a 'making strange' that deforms language and calls attention to itself in the process" proves paradigmatic of the narrow readings late-twentieth-century poetic scholars apply to Shklovsky's concept (Perloff, "How to Read a Poem," unpaginated). For one

also could argue, following Shklovskian premises, that the most defamiliarizing poetry subverts expectation (and thus slows down perceptions) by appearing utterly informal (unchallenging, unnoticeable) within the formal contexts of poetic performance and/or poetic publication. Perloff makes such a case in her 2001 introduction to Dalkey Archive's reprint of David Antin's classic volume *Talking*. More generally, however, and as I will argue in subsequent chapters, critics' single-minded emphases (Perloff's included) upon defamiliarization in its most obvious, syntactical forms has effectively screened works that rely upon what Pop-theorist Lawrence Alloway describes as a vernacular-based "translatability."

4 Here I cannot help but recall Wayne Koestenbaum's astute attention (in the poet/critic's *Andy Warhol* biography) to Warhol's self-imposed nickname "Andy Paperbag." In fact, art-historian Douglas Crimp's description of Warhol's 1965 film *John and Ivy* appears to prefigure the stars, light-bulbs and paper bags of Brainard's own pop-inflected potpourri:

> Some other things Ivy does: she brushes her teeth with a battery-powered toothbrush, smokes, reads the children's books, pulls up the black tights that she wears beneath her over-the-calf boots . . . makes instant coffee, dances to songs by the Shangri-Las and the Beatles playing on the radio, blows air into a paper bag and pops it behind John's head while kissing him, and throws a snowball at John. (6)

5 While I have emphasized *I Remember*'s abrupt shifts in rhetorical register, I do not mean to discount the work's delicate poetic touches: its coordinated assonantal clusters ("Carver . . . cartoon stars"; "light bulbs for a bright idea"); nimble, alliterative phrasings ("peanut butter . . . paper bags"; "blowing up paper bags to pop") and faint, fugitive echoes (a soft-rhyme on "$200" and "butter," for example—an audition further attenuated by the facts that the word "dollars" never appears in Brainard's passage, and that the placement of the dollar symbol *before* its quantifying modifier contradicts our enunciation of the sentence.

6 As if to confirm its departure from dramatic progress, Brainard's Angel Hair Press *I Remember* series contains no page numbers.

7 In his 1970 essay "Early Warhol: The Systematic Evolution of the Impersonal Style," critic/curator/artist John Coplans offers this succinct account of Warhol's "Do It Yourself" series:

> Taken from hobby shop color-keyed painting sets, these banal images are transformed by Warhol into strange paintings that are themselves supremely banal metaphors for paintings . . . The "Do It Yourself' paintings pose the question: can a painting be made that looks mechanical but is not? . . . They mark the first suggestion of Warhol's finding means to expunge entirely the use of the artist's hand from his painting. (53)

8 Lewis Warsh and Tom Clark provide perhaps the most succinct examples of such smart, suggestive analyses:

> He gave the reader the illusion he was telling everything, without getting heavy or going too deep. (Warhol was an early influence and hero). (Warsh, "Brainard," 109)

> Can you imagine another naif genius of such deep trust and sophistication, so good at making (or seeming to make) primitive = advanced, so given to everything, generating so consistently, in a way that looks so almost casual, such an infinitely cool all-over heat of presence, contingency, spectacle, design? (Clark, 99)

9 Again, Warsh and Clark provide concise, appealing accounts:

> I had the feeling that he didn't think about himself that much—that he had figured out a way of taking care of himself and that he could devote his time to taking care of others. (Warsh, "Brainard" 110)

> Back in the days when being poor could still occasionally be fun, Joe's generous donation of marvelous works and designs to flybynight publishing ventures was one of the great taken-for-granted pleasures, as though we all somehow deserved the honor of world-class illustration and cover art simply because the artist was our pal and willing to deliver same at short notice, totally without ado and absolutely gratis. (Clark, 98)

10 Twenty years earlier, Corbett's very different response to *I Re-*

member (a 1980 review for *L=A=N=G=U=A=G=E* magazine, entitled "Seventeen Titles Joe Brainard Will Use One Day") provides a much more playful, more elusive, more Brainardesque assessment:

> I Forgot to Remember
> Boy Scout Cookies
> Truer Words Were Never Said
> A Regular Joe
> Read Any Good Books Lately? (12)

11 I follow poet/critic Maggie Nelson in retaining the "New York School" term, even with its many art-literary-historical ambiguities and limitations, thereby acknowledging that while its definition "may necessarily remain in flux," the term is "not without real referents or pragmatic power" (xviii).

12 The phrase "Saint Joe" derives from Edmund White's 1997 essay of that title. While White's piece deploys this moniker with appropriate camp panache, as a term of affection rather than a tool of interpretation, the saintly rhetoric has lingered in retrospective accounts of Brainard's work ever since. Ron Padgett, for example, concludes his 2004 biography *Joe* by affirming White's designation: "I do know that Joe, with his aversion for inflated pronouncements and his awareness of his own foibles, would hardly have thought that *saintly* applied to him. I just don't know what other word to use" (313).

13 Brainard characteristically traces the self-critical, asymptotic limits to his own "honest" tendencies:

> Brigid Polk said to me last night that I was the most honest person she knew. I wanted to say "No", [sic] but somehow

more than just "No." I don't remember what I said, but this morning I was thinking about it and it came to me what I should have said. That honest is only something you can *try* to be. (If you want to be.) And I do. But I don't want to have to take credit for *being* honest. Because, even if it were possible, it would be too much to have to live up to. Another impossible weight. (*Selected*, 112)

You know, it's really funny this kind of writing. This "trying to be honest" kind of writing. For several years now I've been doing it, and getting better and better at it. Getting closer and closer to a point (a place) in my head I call the truth. But now I'm beginning to doubt that very point. (That very place) (*Bolinas* 27)

14 Brainard's self-appraisal, "Not Intelligent. But smart," from *Selected Writing: 1962-1971*'s "Autobiography" piece, conspicuously echoes Smithson's 1969 description of the Cayuga Salt Mine site as "Not didactic, but dialectic" (Brainard, 121; Smithson, 190).
15 Brainard's delightful renderings of his Bolinas trip merit more extensive citation than I here can provide:

It seems I am always looking for matches. (12)

Small birds do a beautiful thing around here of circling around each other, in pairs, as they drop through space. (23)

Those little white morning glories that grow close to the

> ground looking up. I especially like them. (28)
>
> A little girl wants a quarter. Giving her a nickel she mumbles "motherfucker" and walks away. (32)

16 In fact, Brainard's probing public record of his relationship with Elmslie—emblematic of a generalized ambivalence towards potential care-givers: relatives ("I remember my grandfather who lived on a farm dunking his cornbread in his buttermilk. He didn't like to talk"); immediate predecessors ("I remember painting 'I HATE TED BERRIGAN' in big black letters all over my white wall"); and Bolinas' many kind hosts—serves as testament to Elmslie's prodigious patience, as much as to Brainard's unflinching "honesty" (Brainard, *I Remember*, 15, 5). Consider, for instance, this swift, gratuitous-seeming follow-up to the Elmslie passages cited above:

> "Tuesday December 30th, 1971"
> That Kenward is the only person I can sing in front of, IS love tonight, even if it isn't.*
>
> * What a prick I am! (*New*, 48)

17 According to Victor Bockris' biography *Transformer: The Lou Reed Story*, Warhol told Reed he should write a song about someone vicious. When Reed asked what he meant, Warhol replied, "Oh, you know, vicious, like I hit you with a flower" (200).

18 As subsequent chapters of this book make clear, I adopt the phrase "Pop poetics" in order to analyze numerous methodological affinities (including indexical/appropriative generation, additive construction, serial composition, etc.) among a particular group of postwar artists and poets. I do not mean to suggest that Brainard, Schuyler, and Myles self-consciously constructed a Pop poetry movement founded on, for instance, Warholian paradigms, but rather to demonstrate that the rich art-historical discourse on this era has much to offer literary scholars. By focusing on Joe Brainard as an exemplar of Pop poetics, I mean to outline a broader exchange among Post-Ab Ex innovators, yet to depart from what poet/scholar Michael Davidson describes as a "familiar school-based criticism" which "presumes group agreement on certain shared aesthetic tenets and ignores the fruitful role of dissension, disagreement, panic and erotic play that underlie group formation" (18). My own extended study will remain devoted to Brainard's undertheorized corpus, and I will leave it to subsequent scholars to apply related arguments to the output of Brainard's close friends, if that ever seems a worthwhile enterprise.

19 Even the cover of Padgett's scrupulous memoir *Joe* portrays its subject perched between heaven and earth: posing somewhat awkwardly upon a Manhattan fire escape (in tie, v-neck sweater, Chuck Taylor's, tube socks), amid stairs ascending towards the empty white sky.

20 Certainly other types of tribute appear in this *Pressed Wafer* volume. A third way, for example—a combination of the conceptual and retrospective tendencies outlined above—emerges in Ed Barrett's and Anselm Berrigan's comedic variations on

Brainard's "I Remember" form. In "The Living End," Barrett literalizes the gaps of attention implied throughout Brainard's aphoristic text:

> I forget the words to the lullaby my father made up which began *ritchie ritchie roona* . . . . . .
>
> I forget when Patrick Barrett, who came over from Ireland, erected the family headstone in Holy Cross Cemetery. 1838 or 1878 . . .
>
> I have two middle names (Charles William) and I forget who the Charles is I was named after. (147-148)

In "I remember hearing Joe read," Berrigan offers a serialized, essayistic variant on typical free-verse recollection:

> I remember hearing Joe Brainard read his poem
> "I remember"
> at the Ear Inn when I was eight or nine years old.
>
> I remember that of all the poets I had heard read
> up to that point
> Joe was not only the best, but the only one who
> was any good at all. (212)

Along similar lines, it is not Brainard's immediate peers, but his younger admirer, poet Jerome Sala, who provides *Pressed Wafer's* most expansive analytic account—one that attempts to synthesize Brainard's retrospective and conceptualist tendencies:

> Take I Remember. On the one hand, it's so ordinary that pre-literate people (little kids) can enjoy It—and learn to read and write from it. On the other, the 'work' I Remember is a highly complex, conceptual piece of literary art—one that explores the wild variations found in sameness; and that stacks weighty discourses atop one another—from oral history, to cultural criticism to identity politics—with an offhand grace and wit that would seem shockingly authentic, if the whole notion of authenticity weren't thrown into question by its ultra-cool aesthetic. (130)

21 Again, to his credit, Corbett, as *Pressed Wafer* editor (with poets Elaine Equi and David Trinidad serving as guest editors on the Brainard issue), must have recognized the value in such experimentally inclined accounts.

22 Published as part of *New Work*'s "Selections from N.Y.C. Journals 1971 & 1972" sequence, "Neck" contains such quintessential Brainard observations as:

> One thing I've noticed is that I tilt my head a lot in bars. If tilting my head "means" anything, I don't think it means anything very important. (41)

23 Brainard indents each *I Remember* entry's first line (suggest-

ing paragraph format), whereas Trinidad reverses this arrangement (suggesting poetic lineation).

24 I will address Brainard's relation to Cage in subsequent chapters. Brainard's affinity with Cornell's composite mode of construction appears most clearly, perhaps, in this only surviving excerpt from the poet's projected verbal-portrait series:

> *Jimmy Schuyler*
> Trees. Baby blue. Plaid. Pajamas. Leather. Wrist watch. Pocket knife. Books. Silver. Autumn. Coffee. Scissors. Yellow. Lima beans. Belt. (Padgett, 199)

25 As will become clear in later chapters, the centripetal/centrifugal tensions present throughout Brainard's oeuvre crystallize here, as the attentive artist breaks through one self-imposed frame, only to emerge encompassed by a slightly more expansive template—a sheet of stamped, cropped paper.

26 In her 2008 article "Sincerity and the Second Person: Lyric after Language Poetry," critic Jennifer Ashton has sought to push beyond such reductive binaries, by presenting her own work as "an effort to understand the simultaneous emergence of two striking trends in U.S. poetry during the past decade":

> 1) the popularity of appropriative techniques (e.g., collage, cross-outs, or . . . transcription) and 2) new imperatives to construct poems that appear to resist artifice, whether in the form of commitment to sincerity, a lick of irony, a childlike innocence or wonder, artlessness, etc . . . The problem set recurs in a number of guises: in the efforts to differentiate,

> for example, between poems that emphasize the "personal" and those that announce their "impersonality"; between a speaker's sincerity or authenticity, or between either of these and their imagined impossibility; between denying and asserting the poem's relation to a reader/ listener/ audience. In short, a set of problems that epitomize the kinds of projects we commonly identify either with lyric as such or with its critique. (94)

I would add that Pop poetics, especially serialized, first-person projects such as Brainard's, anticipate many of the trends that Ashton detects in our own present.

27 In the late twentieth-century, Russell Ferguson's *In Memory of My Feelings: Frank O'Hara and American Art* (1999) and Reva Wolf's *Andy Warhol, Poetry, and Gossip in the 1960s* (1997) provided laudable exceptions to these scholarly aporia. Yet here it is worth noting that Ferguson (at the time an art curator) and Wolf (an art-historian) stood outside the confines of poetic discourse proper. More recently, Maggie Nelson's *Women, the New York School, and Other True Abstractions* (Iowa City: University of Iowa, 2007) has provided an exemplary account of conceptualist poetic practices in individual works by Mayer and Notley, and Michael S. Hennessey's "An Imperfect Diamond: The National Pastime Transfigured in Ted Berrigan and Harris Schiff's *Yo-Yo's with Money*" (*Interval(le)s* 4/5, 2009) has done the same for Berrigan and Schiff.

28 Of course, Brainard's Pop-inflected word play differs from that of his language-based peers:

I remember "Korea." (58)

I remember "Uranium." (97)

I remember *Kon-Tiki*. (97)

29 Some Brainard aficionados may declare their indifference to this beloved poet's status amid "academic" debate. But then the overall purpose of a Brainard tribute (is it really just to swap stories and encourage new *I Remember* knockoffs?) remains to be specified.
30 Padgett himself pointed me to the *Art of Assemblage* catalogue during an interview conducted in 2005.
31 Again, Padgett's recollections prove apropos:

> Joe's work at the time (1963-1964) was mostly assemblages and collages, involving, as he put it in an unpublished interview I did with him:
>
> > ice cream cones and spiders and nails and feathers and cigarette butts and roses and orchids and flamingo birds and cardinal birds and blue birds and blue ferns and dancing girls and skeletons and fringe and tassels and lace and linoleum and ribbon and Dristan and toothpaste and the Infant Jesus of Prague . . . [Brainard's list continues for about 20 more lines] (69)
>
> The [1965] show [at the Alan Gallery contained]: approximately seventeen glittering, outrageous as-

> semblages of bright pink rubber snakes, plastic flowers, crucifixes, lobster claws, Lucky Strike packages, a moose statuette, rosaries, costume jewels, bowties covered with glitter . . . [Padgett's list continues for 6 more lines] (80)

> In February [1966] he asked Pat and me to save our cigarette butts and mail them to him for use in the small assemblages he was making, usually a solid group of butts around a central object. The previous month he had asked us to be on the lookout for hands—from mannequins, on postcards . . . (102)

32 In doing so, Seitz helps to consolidate what Robert Rosenblum describes as a burgeoning "international movement in the late 1950s that would explore, whether in the New York of Robert Rauschenberg and Louise Nevelson or the Paris of Arman and Jacques de la Villegé, the strange new poetry that could be eked out of the palatable junk and mess of urban life" (*Aquarius*, xiv).

33 Here again, I do not mean to discount the value of Abstract Expressionist painting/New York School poetry juxtapositions, so much as to assert the need for literary scholars to progress beyond familiar references to the first two decades of postwar art. Within this context, Seitz's blockbuster "Assemblage" show (self-consciously pitched as epoch-shaping event for a generation both "weaned on abstract expressionism but unwilling to mannerize Pollock [or] de Kooning," and inspired by a proto-

Pop "impatience with the line that separated art from life") offers just one of myriad points of departure for post-Ab Ex art/poetry comparisons (Seitz, 87).

34 Here Seitz's claim that assemblage art "disturbed supporters of both figurative and abstract art" anticipates Warhol's now-legendary impact upon postwar painting, but also Brainard's less-celebrated impact upon postwar poetry (32).

35 Gooch's prescient attention to "how *conceptual* Brainard was" has informed my own sense of the artist (127).

36 As is often the case with Brainard's writing, Andy Warhol here serves as inescapable point of reference, though Brainard's own deployment of the "So what" phrase precedes Warhol's treatise on the subject—from 1975's *Philosophy of Andy Warhol: From A to B and Back Again*:

> Sometimes people let the same problems make them miserable for years when they should just say, "So what." That's one of my favorite things to say. "So what."
> "My mother didn't love me." So what.
> "My husband won't ball me." So what.
> "I'm a success but I'm still all alone." So what.
> I don't know how I made it through all the years before I learned to do that trick. (112)

37 Schuyler's "Under the Hanger" takes its lines from the journals of eighteenth-century naturalist Gilbert White.

38 Scholars outside of art history often understate Pop art's epistemically minded critique of postwar industrial/aesthetic

production. In his 1968 response to Andy Warhol's work, critic/curator/artist John Coplans offers this succinct account of Pop as a pointed, conceptually driven enterprise:

> Implicit to all [of Warhol's] images is a contradiction among the origin of the imagery, the various mechanical and industrial processes used in their facture, and what finally emerges as a work of art. Warhol enforces the issue that the range of esthetic judgments necessary to create a work of art are of the mind and not the hand. (130)

39 Spatial limitations prevent me from providing a more comprehensive account of Language discourse's longstanding tendency toward self-differentiation from mainstream or lyric poetry. For a brief survey of early, influential statements by Language-affiliated poets, see Bruce Andrews, "Text and Context," Charles Bernstein, "Stray Straws and Straw Men," Steve McCaffery, "The Death of the Subject," and Ron Silliman, "For Open Letter" (all reprinted in *L=A=N=G=U=A=G=E*, Supplement Number One [June 1980]); Ron Silliman, Barrett Watten, Steve Benson, Lyn Hejinian, Charles Bernstein & Bob Perelman, "For Change," (reprinted in *In the American Tree* [Orono, Maine: National Poetry Foundation, 1986]), 484-490; Ron Silliman, Carla Harryman, Lyn Hejinian, Steve Benson, Bob Perelman, & Barrett Watten, "Aesthetic Tendency and the Politics of Poetry: A Manifesto," *Social Text*, No. 19/20 (Autumn, 1988), 261-275. For more recent, retrospective analyses of Language poetry's response to lyric subjectivity, see Ron Silliman, "Who Speaks: Ventriloquism and the Self

in the Poetry Reading," *Close Listening: Poetry and the Performed Word* (New York: Oxford University Press, 1998) 360-378; Steve McCaffery, "Insufficiency of Theory to Poetical Economy," *Prior to Meaning: the Protosemantic and Poetics* (Evanston, Il: Northwestern University Press, 2001) 3-14; Marjorie Perloff "Language Poetry and the Lyric Subject," and "After Language Poetry: Innovation and its Theoretical Discontents," *Differentials: Poetry, Poetics, Pedagogy* (Tuscaloosa: University of Alabama Press, 2004) 129-174.

40 Especially within the twenty-first century, Perloff has attempted to question Language's "oppositional" pose. Yet Perloff's own studies have continued to glamorize Language's oppositional ethos—if only by reinforcing the movement's paradigmatic position as paragon of late-twentieth-century avant-garde experiment. Thus even Perloff's calls for renewed explorations of post-war poetic subjecthood seem to take for granted that these new approaches will privilege Language texts:

> It was, of course, the opposition to [the] Romantic paradigm that prompted the theoretical discourse of Language manifestos in the first place. And that oppositionality remains significant even though the "Us-versus-Them" rhetoric of *The L=A=N =G=U=A=G=E Book*, now twenty years old, has become complicated by the appearance of new poetic paradigms that don't quite fit the original theoretical frame. The dialectic, in other words, has shifted ground and it now seems more useful to look at special cases *within* the Language movement

> and related alternate poetries rather than at the group phenomenon. (*Differentials*, 153)

41 In this book's introduction I discuss the problematic role that personalized responses from Brainard's friends have played in subsequent accounts of this artist/poet's aesthetic output. Here, I mean to suggest that Brainard's supporters should not be faulted for this unfortunate situation, since their continued advocacy serves to fill a vacuum left by uninterested critics. Similarly, of course—and to shift my vantage beyond the scope of this particular chapter—no one experimentally inclined scholar, such as Marjorie Perloff, should be expected to recognize and validate each and every significant poetic innovation of the postwar era. In critiquing Perloff's work, I remain very much aware of her catalyzing contributions to contemporary poetic criticism, as well as of the broader marginalization of postwar poetics that she has artfully resisted.

42 As I am completing this manuscript, in 2010, new opportunities have arisen to reconsider female artists in a Pop movement long considered exclusionary of women and/or misogynist. For a concise account of these recent developments, see artist Carrie Moyer's review (in the April, 2010 edition of *Artforum International*) of the "Seductive Subversion: Women Pop Artists 1958-68" show at the University of the Arts' Rosenwald-Wolf Gallery in Philadelphia.

43 Of course, literature and literary studies stimulate artistic and art-historical projects as well. Krauss, for example, frequently acknowledges her indebtedness to Roland Barthes and Jacques Derrida. Here my point is simply that art historians swiftly apply

poststructuralist analyses to Pop paintings, whereas literary critics fail to do so with Pop poems.

44 Consider, for example, poet Steve McCaffery's opening to 1977's Language-galvanizing "Politics of the Referent" symposium:

> As we understand increasingly the unity of the human symbolic field and how man is primarily a semiotic animal inhabiting and creating a context that is itself semiotic and governed by common operations, as we understand this so we will understand how the whole notion of a literature discriminated from language is irrelevant. ("Subject" 2)

45 In his 1996 *The Return of the Real* volume, for example, Hal Foster considers Warhol within the greater context of a resurgent avant-garde tradition derived from Duchamp and Dada. Buchloh does the same in his 1989 essay "Andy Warhol's One-Dimensional Art: 1956-1966."

46 I cite Roy Campbell's 1952 translation of Baudelaire's stanza:

> En vain j'ai voulu de l'espace
> Trouver la fin et le milieu;
> Sous je ne sais quel oeil de feu
> Je sens mon aile qui se casse; (218)

Campbell's *Fleurs du Mal* famously deviates from Baudelaire's text, but here Campbell's emphasis upon geographical coordinates helps to clarify Baudelaire's allegorical traversal of poetic space.

47 Within a more contemporary context, poet Clark Coolidge's dictionary-definition opening to his 1970 volume *Space* proves pertinent:

SPACE

(spās), n. O.F. espace, fr. L. spatium space.

> 1. That which is characterized by extension in all directions, boundlessness, and indefinite divisibility; the subject of determinations of position and direction. 2. Math. The aggregate of points, or ordered sets of n numbers (x1, . . . xn). 3. A limited extension in one, two, or three dimensions: a part marked off in some way. 4. Specif., reservation; accommodations, as on a train. 5. An interval between two points of time; duration. 6. Opportunity; chance. 7. Archaic. A while. 8. Advertising. The page or part of a page of a periodical used for advertising, or the number of agate lines so used in a newspaper. Trade Slang, U.S . . . —*v.t.*; SPACED (spāst); SPAĆING (spāsing). To place at intervals; to arrange with spaces between. (1)

48 For the sake of analogical clarity I am offering a somewhat simplified version of Krauss's argument. In her essay "The Originality of the Avant-Garde," Krauss does in fact detect a continuously reduplicated pictorial scene, the trope of "the frame" itself—as this reappears from Renaissance optics manuals, to Symbolist windows, to modernist grids.

49 Howe herself describes "Thorow" as a temporal "landscape":

> I think I was trying to paint a landscape in that poem but my vision of the lake [Lake George] was not so much in space as in time. I was very much aware of the commercialization and near ruin at the edge of the water, in the town itself, all around—but I felt outside of time or in an earlier time and that was what I wanted to get on paper. (Beckett, 20)

John Cage's swirling "Talk I" (reprinted in 1967's *A Year from Monday*) also might have served as model.

50 Of course, one could argue that these works do not destroy meaning by breaking up sentences, but rather construct meanings through novel combinations of syntactic units. I address this tension between additive/subtractive, centripetal/centrifugal processes in a subsequent chapter entitled "Serial Sixties: Monet, Warhol, Brainard." For now, I am simply expanding upon Mallarmé's advocacy of poetic "dispersal."

51 Again, I do not aim to present McCaffery's early analysis as representative of this astute poet/critic's entire career. Nor do I mean to suggest that McCaffery's statements can stand in for Language discourse as a whole. In her 1999 essay "After Language Poetry: Innovation and its Theoretical Discontents," Marjorie Perloff ably articulates the disparate philosophical and aesthetic orientations that early Language practitioners brought to the movement:

> McCaffery himself points to the Russian Formalists, to

> Wittgenstein, Barthes, Lacan, and Derrida as the sources for his theory, and indeed language poetics, in this first stage, owes its greatest debt to French poststructuralism, although Charles Bernstein, for one, was much closer to Wittgenstein, whom he had studied with Stanley Cavell at Harvard, than to Derrida, whose analysis of signification he distrusted, even as Silliman and Andrews were drawn to a more politicized Frankfurt School poetics. (*Differentials*, 158)

Within my own account, it is McCaffery's quasi-pictorial emphasis upon the grapheme that makes his work so fitting for discussions of late-modernist poetic space.

52 Krauss offers this description in response to early-fifties artistic paradigms, which suggests the comparative belatedness of "subjectless" Language abstractions.

53 Here and elsewhere, Nietzsche's avowed enthusiasm for Emerson's essays (Nietzsche's "genealogical" approach often appears a direct extension of Emerson's "fossil poetry" concept), hints at latent affinities between the former's perspectival "scientist," and the latter's prototypical American poet/scholar.

54 The italics are, as usual, Nietzsche's.

55 In this book's introduction I make reference to a nearby sequence of early entries from *I Remember*:

> I remember the only time I ever saw my mother cry. I was eating apricot pie.
> I remember how much I cried seeing "South Pacific" (the

> movie) three times.
> I remember how good a glass of water can taste after a dish of ice cream. (2)

56 Along similar lines, art-historian Robert Rosenblum's mid-sixties description of Pop painting helps to demonstrate the charged correspondence between readymade detail and quasi-autobiographical record in Pop poetics:

> The authentic Pop artist offers a coincidence of style and subject, that is, he represents mass-produced images and objects by using a style which is also based upon the visual vocabulary of mass production. ("Pop," 81)

Critic Lawrence Alloway's concurrent description of Pop "anonymity" points toward the writerly implications of such personal/impersonal poems:

> Where process abbreviation is found in Pop Art it reduces personal nuances of handling by the artist in favour of deadpan or passive images. This deceptive impersonality amounts to a game with anonymity, a minimizing of invention, so that the work is free to support its interconnections with popular culture, and with the shared world of the spectator. (20)

And John Ashbery's subsequent commentary upon James Schuyler's corpus (along with Schuyler's praise for David Trinidad's work) rounds out a rough sketch of the multivalent "translatability" (the potential for vernacular-based abstractions *to return to* the world of vernacular discourse) that Alloway deems so crucial to Pop projects:

> [Schuyler] somehow managed to draw on the whole arsenal of modernism, from the minimalism of Dr. Williams to the gorgeous aberrations of Wallace Stevens and the French Surrealists, and still write in what Marianne Moore calls "plain American which cats and dogs can read." (209)
>
> The case of Trinidad's lines and the colloquial care with which he chooses words—precise, without knocking you down—are the means he uses to create these so original poems: intense, yet off the cuff: turning the paste jewels of pop art into the real thing: which might be, to leave them as he found them, shining, and singing about a broken heart (perhaps). (Book cover)

57 Within this context, even Barthes's pronouncement of the author's death served less to consolidate a deconstructionist epoch, than to ensure that "the game started over again" (just as, following his "Death of the Author" publication, Barthes himself began to master the autobiographical form).

58 For further questions concerning hybridized form, consider Michel Delville's *The American Prose Poem: Poetic Form and the Boundaries of Genre* (Gainesville: University of Florida Press, 1998). For an expanded conception of twentieth-century poetic experiment, see Craig Dworkin's *Reading the Illegible* (Evanston:

Northwestern University Press, 2003).

59 Of course, Perloff's and Conte's critical theses do not stop with the texts cited above. To readers familiar with the former's career, for instance, it may be interesting to note that "From Image to Action's" publication date places it between Perloff's 1970's revaluations of the modern lyric tradition (from Yeats to Robert Lowell to Frank O'Hara), and her subsequent emphasis upon marginalized modernist and postmodernist poetries (in texts such as 1985's *The Dance of the Intellect: Studies in the Poetry of the Pound Tradition*, 1986's *The Futurist Moment: Avant-Garde, Avant Guerre, and the Language of Rupture* and beyond). Conte likewise updates his conceptions of serial poetry, and of poetic abstraction, in a 1992 article "Seriality and the Contemporary Long Poem," in 1997's "The Smooth and the Striated: Texture in the Modern Long Poem," and in his editorship of the *Dictionary of Literary Biography* (particularly in the critic's own James Schuyler entry). Again, I do not desire to blame Perloff and Conte for present gaps in poetic scholarship, but rather to demonstrate how influential each critic's early formulations remain.

60 Pound and Eliot prove, at best, "exceptions to the rule: both *The Waste Land* and the *Cantos* are full of abortive stories, tales fragmented and never fully developed that weave in and out of the lyric fabric" (Perloff, *Dance*, 156).

61 Defining *gnosis*, Perloff quotes Victor Turner's etymology of the term "narration"—from his 1980 essay "Social Dramas and Stories about Them":

> Narrate is from the Latin *narrare* ('to tell') which is akin to the Latin *gna[~]rus* ('knowing,' 'acquainted with,' 'expert

> in') both derivative from the Indo-European root *gna[^]* ('to know') whence the vast family of words deriving from the Latin *cognoscere*, including 'cognition' itself, and 'noun' and 'pronoun,' the Greek *gigno[~]kein*, whence *gno[~]sis*. (Turner, 164)

62 Perloff problematizes the neo-Romantic obfuscation of post-industrial social conditions most effectively in her book-length project *Radical Artifice: Writing Poetry in the Age of Media* (Chicago: University of Chicago Press, 1991).

63 More generally, Perloff's "Action" concept seems analogous to the medium-specific interventions of a preceding generation's "action" (Abstract Expressionist) painters—suggesting the extent to which "From Image to Action" (and subsequent critics' extensions of its arguments) still looks back to late-modernist aesthetics, thereby marginalizing postwar Pop innovation.

64 Perloff, writing in 1982, refers to the 1975 version of Dorn's epic—a multi-volume work begun with 1968's *Gunslinger*, and completed by 1989's *Gunslinger*.

65 For an intriguing account of these texts, see Mark Ford's essay "Like a Lily Daché Hat" (*Poetry Review* [Autumn 2002]).

66 Here I follow the late-twentieth-century dandy's lineage, as traced by Susan Sontag's classic essay, "Notes on Camp":

> The dandy was overbred. His posture was disdain, or else ennui. He sought rare sensations, undefiled by mass appreciation . . . He was dedicated to "good taste."
>
> The connoisseur of Camp has found more ingenious

> pleasures . . . Camp—Dandyism in the age of mass culture—makes no distinction between the unique object and the mass-produced object. Camp taste transcends the nausea of the replica. (289)

67 *New Work*'s placement of "30 One-Liners" between a statement entitled "Saturday, June 10th, 1972" and a piece named "What I Did this Summer" makes it a very near contemporary indeed to Elderfield's May, 1972, *Artforum* article.

68 Dorn's publication-by-installment strategy (not unlike Brainard's own, with the *I Remember, I Remember More, More I Remember More* sequence) confirms that *Slinger* simultaneously could be read for its additive propensities.

69 Separate studies ought to address the literary-historical dynamic by which white, straight, male authors have remained the most celebrated poetic "rebels" during a cultural epoch largely defined by race-, gender- and sexuality-specific liberation movements (Perloff makes this point in her "After Language Poetry" essay, as does Nelson in *Women, the New York School, and Other True Abstractions*). For my own part, though I do not wish to essentialize connections between homosexuality, Camp praxis and/or serial poetics, I find a propitious point of departure for examining relations among gay, Camp and serial sensibilities to be Roland Barthes's *Roland Barthes* entry "The Goddess H":

> The pleasure potential of a perversion (in this case, that of the two H's: homosexuality and hashish) is always underestimated. Law, Science, the *Doxa* refuse to understand that perversion, quite simply, *makes happy*; or

> to be more specific, it produces a *more*: I am more sensitive, more perceptive, more loquacious, more amused, etc.—and in this *more* is where we find the difference (and, consequently, the Text of Life, life-as-text). (64)

Whereas parody, in Perloff's sense, suggests a zero-sum game (one perspective's enhancement at another's expense), Camp and additive composition nimbly accrue the "*more*" that Barthes finds so appealing.

70 Nor does the case for Pop poetry's contemporaneous place alongside a more familiar "serial poetics" rest solely on theoretical grounds. Brainard and Creeley collaborated on 1973's *The Class of '47* text, for example, and Brainard's 1971 *Bolinas Journal* discusses the poet's social engagements with Creeley and Duncan.

71 The term "anaphora" appears not once, for instance, in Conte's 300-page study.

72 In his 1987 study *Postmodernist Fiction*, for example, critic Brian McHale categorizes Robbe-Grillet's later novels (beginning with 1965's *La Maison de rendezvous*) as "nouveau nouveau" romans that can serve as "exemplary postmodernist text[s]" (13). Yet McHale considers Robbe-Grillet's earlier, "'classic'" nouveaux romans (such as 1957's *La Jalousie*) "stylized modernist novels."

73 Campbell's produced four limited-edition, Warhol-inspired cans in 2004.

74 In fact, part of what seems so lacking in Brainard's ur-*I Remember* ("Gold and Silver and Purple Memories") project is this text's ability to function not just as idiosyncratic, solipsistic record, but as dream-diary of the undifferentiated mass. Paradoxically, it is only when *I Remember*'s persistent "I" gets systemati-

cally integrated into the serial text that Brainard's Pop-inflected litany invokes a vox populi.

75 Though ostensibly concerned with "Russian conditions," Benjamin's "Author as Producer" text cites Bertolt Brecht's *Umfunktionierung* (functional transformation) concept as the theoretical basis for its productivist model (774). Spatial limitations prohibit me from presenting a more elaborate comparison between Brecht's Epic theater and Brainard's Pop-inflected poetic assemblages, but Benjamin's illuminating analysis of the former enterprise prompts a quick juxtaposition:

> Brecht fell back on the most primitive elements of the theater. He contented himself, by and large, with a podium . . . Epic Theater, he declared, had to portray situations, rather than develop plots . . . The interruption of action, on account of which Brecht described his theater as "epic," constantly counteracts illusion on the part of the audience. (778)

What postwar poetic project emphasizes spare, situation-based plot interruption more systematically than Brainard's *I Remember*?

76 In his 1978-79 "Day by Day with Roland Barthes" project, Barthes describes the "soft form" as possessing "neither the solemnity of the maxim, nor the harshness of the epigram; something which, at least in tendency, might suggest the Japanese haiku, the Joycean epiphany, the fragment of the *journal intime*" (116).

77 Here I do not mean to diminish the hostile response that Language discourse long received from academic audiences, nor to deny the proletarian origins and/or political commitments of cer-

tain Language practitioners. The irony, however, is that this movement's overall trajectory closely resembles what the young Ron Silliman describes as modernism's "defensive" rise to prominence:

> The 'art of the difficult' aspect of modernism is a defensive mechanism. By difficulty, a writer made it harder to be absorbed and commoditized. It is a form of buying time. It is a sad thing to watch. It never works. ("Open," 33)

Within this context, Brainard's "art of the simple" approach has proved much more effective at resisting absorption and commoditization.

78 Admittedly, the voluminous supplemental discourse that has sprung up around Language poems constricts the range of potential reader-response.

79 In this most famous of his works, the author admits, "I remember taking an I.Q. test and coming out below average. (I've never told anybody that before)" (49).

80 Perloff posits seriality's defamiliarizing, "'demilitarizing'" syntax in her 1997 piece "The Music of Verbal Space: John Cage's 'What You Say'" (*Emergent*, 299).

81 Each of these texts gained prominence amid Brainard's New York art-world milieu. Oldenburg's "I am for an art" litany derived from the artist's 1961-62 downtown-based installation/performance "The Store." Albers' "The Origin of Art"—first printed in a 1952 issue of the Parisian journal *Réalités Nouvelles*—resurfaced in MoMA's 1964 volume *Homage to the Square*. Reinhardt's 1966 "There is Just One Painting" statement appeared in *Artforum*.

82 I follow Conte in taking the "quick graph" phrase from Cree-

ley's 1970 volume *A Quick Graph: Collected Notes and Essays.*
83 In his 1998 essay "A Fan's Apostasy," Wayne Koestenbaum offers an analogous assimilation of the anaphoric phrase into critical prose:

> I am interested in the opera of driving a car, the opera of taking the subway, the opera of deferred gratification, the opera of massage parlors, the opera of sunset at the piers, the opera of whisky, the opera of silence, the opera of palm trees, the opera of bath tubs, the opera of the daily splash of eau de cologne, the opera of inanition, the opera of stupefaction, the opera of amnesia. (*Cleavage*, 195).

84 I take these respective passages from Howe's *Frame Structures: Early Poems, 1974-1979*, Siliman's *The Age of Huts (Compleat)*, and Bernstein's *Girly Man*.
85 Critic Mary Ann Caws seems to suggest as much about Brainard's serializing precursor Walt Whitman, whose "Song of Myself" she wisely includes in her 2001, modernist-based anthology *Manifesto: A Century of Isms*.
86 I take these and every subsequent manifesto citation from Caws's *Manifesto* anthology.
87 Conte takes this phrase from Roland Barthes's 1962 "The Imagination of the Sign" essay.
88 Quartermain's concise genealogy hints, alas, at its own limited range of reference, refraining to ask, for example, whether any number of epistolary and/or aphoristic practices (cyclic ruminations by Epictetus and Marcus Aurelius, collaborative renga by thirteenth-century Japanese poets, Montaigne's essays, seventeenth-century commonplace books, quasi-indexical catalogues by

Dorothy Wordsworth and John Clare, philosophical meditations by Nietzsche, Wittgenstein, Bataille, Benjamin, Weil, Barthes—the list could fill an entire volume) have not contributed to a proto-serial poetics of "contiguously related particulars" (Conte, 91).

89 For a broad introduction to related work on Dickinson's fascicles, see also Martha Nell Smith's article "Rowing in Eden: Reading Dickinson Reading" (printed in *Rowing in Eden: Rereading Emily Dickinson* [Austin: University of Texas Press, 1992]), and the transcript from the Emily Dickinson International Society's 1997 roundtable discussion "Unfastening the Fascicles" (including works by scholars Robert Bray, Paul James Crumbley, Eleanor Elson Heginbotham, and Daneen Leigh Wardrop—and available through the emilydickinson.org website).

90 Sixty years earlier, in his classic *The American Renaissance* text, F.O. Matthiessen entitled his main Whitman chapter "Only a Language Experiment," yet treated this resonant phrase as authenticity-affirming confirmation that "a man cannot use words so unless he has experienced the facts that they express" (518). For a more recent, book-length meditation upon Whitman's statement, see James Perrin Warren's *Walt Whitman's Language Experiment* (University Park: Pennsylvania State University, 1990).

91 This decade-long tension between casual/inclusive, and austere/exclusive accounts of serial composition manifests most clearly, perhaps, in two 1967 articles by painters David Lee ("Serial Rights") and Mel Bochner ("The Serial Attitude"):

> The [serial] attitude is that there are all these parts to everything, that every part is interesting, but that there is not much interest in any one part . . . A series is a way of

viewing one's experience and a way of representing one's view. By "experience" I mean daily life. This and this and this; one thing after another. (Lee, 44)

Many artists work "in series." That is, they make different versions of a basic theme . . . . . . This falls outside the area of concern here. Three basic operating assumptions separate serially ordered works from multiple variants:

1. The derivation of the terms or interior divisions of the work is by means of a numerical or otherwise systematically predetermined process (permutation, progression, rotation, reversal).
2. The order takes precedence over the execution.
3. The completed work is fundamentally parsimonious and systematically self-exhausting. (Bochner, 28)

Bochner's *Artforum* piece offers the more precise, more erudite argument: replete with citations from Ludwig Wittgenstein, Arnold Schoenberg, Milton Babbit, etc. Lee's less-fastidious definition of the "serial attitude"—published that same month in *Art News* (each essay examined the December "Art in Series" show at Finch College)—lends itself to more promiscuous application. Both approaches prove germane to my own analysis of Pop-inflected poetry's chatty tone and quasi-algorithmic structure.

92 Art-historians often position Coplans' 1968 "Serial Imagery" exhibition as a crucial event for reinvigorating curatorial and scholarly concerns with serial design. Critic Christine Mehring, however, has recently pointed out the importance of a

precursor to Coplans' show: 1967's Serielle Formationen exhibition, held at Frankfurt's Johann Wolfgang Goethe Universität, in its Studio Galerie, during May 1967, and curated by artist Peter Roehr and his partner, Paul Maenz. For a compelling introduction to this exhibition, see "Public Options: Christine Mehring on the art of Charlotte Posenenske" (*Artforum International*: Sept. 2010, 273-281).

93 Whether a 32-page Angel Hair Press production, or a 138-page Penguin classic, *I Remember* (published in distinct, self-sufficient stages from 1970-75) relies upon a single, anaphoric phrase, and retains its original introduction and conclusion, thereby illustrating Coplans' claims concerning elastic serial process: "Once established, a Series may be kept open and added to periodically in the future" (11).

94 Fans of New York School poetics may assume that Brainard picks up a brash, vernacular, queer-inflected idiom from his elder friend Frank O'Hara, but a careful reading of Brainard's early output confirms a continuity of tone from his early days as a "below average" high-school student to his subsequent triumphs as a New York artist.

95 Here I feel compelled to point out the curious fact that only when Brainard's text gets placed in properly indented MLA-format does it appear systematically serial. As published in *Selected Writings*, Brainard's repeated assertions do not line up in neat columns (though they do resound, nonetheless, with the vacuous insistence of a preceding decade's "I like Ike" buttons).

96 Hal Foster, for example, in his 1995 essay "The Crux of Minimalism," places Monet at the start of an art-historical tra-

jectory extending from plein air landscape painting to postwar serial production:

> Of course seriality precedes minimalism and pop. Indeed, this procedure penetrated art when its old transcendental orders (God, pristine nature, Platonic forms, artistic genius) began to fall apart. For once the orders were lost as referents or guarantees, "the oeuvre [became] the original" and "each painting [became] a discontinuous term of an indefinite series, and thus legible first not in its relation to the world but in its relation to other paintings by the same artist." Such seriality is not evident much before industrial production, which more than any other force eroded the old orders of art, especially pristine nature. Ironically, even as artists from Claude Monet to Jackson Pollock wrested original impressions from this reified nature, they succumbed to seriality through this very struggle. This succumbing to seriality is fundamental to the becoming abstract of art. (62-63)

Foster takes his quotation from Jean Baudrillard's *From a Critique of the Political Economy of the Sign*, as translated by Charles Levin (St. Louis: Telos Press, 1981).

97 In his 1957 piece, "The Later Monet," critic Clement Greenberg announces this long-neglected artist's nascent rehabilitation:

> Monet is beginning to receive his due . . . An avant-garde painter like André Masson and a critic like Gaston

> Bachelard write about him admiringly. A collector of very modern art in Pittsburgh concentrates on his later works, and the prices of these are rising again. Even more important, their influence is felt—whether directly or indirectly—in some of the most advanced painting now being done in this country. (*Collected*, 3)

Yet Greenberg's attention to Monet's proto-Abstract Expressionist "flat effects," and "chromatic, 'symphonic' structure'" sounds dated once placed beside Seitz's prescient study of Monet's architectonic (and proto-Pop) serial designs (3, 10).

98 Art-historian Rosalind Krauss's 1982 "Photography's Discursive Spaces" essay offers a succinct account of Monet's swift progress from investigations of the picture plane to interrogations of the gallery space:

> The transformation of landscape after 1860 into a flattened and compressed experience of space spreading laterally across the surface was extremely rapid . . . No sooner had this compression occurred, constituting within the single easel painting a representation of the very space of exhibition, than other means of composing were employed: serial landscapes, hung in succession, mimed the horizontal extension of the wall, as in Monet's Rouen Cathedral paintings; or landscapes, compressed and horizonless, expanded to become the absolute size of the wall. The symphony of landscape and wall (the one a representation of the other) of Monet's late

> waterlillies is thus an advanced moment in a series of operations in which aesthetic discourse resolves itself around a representation of the very space that grounds it institutionally. (*Originality*, 133)

99 The press release for MoMA's 2007 "William Seitz: Defending the Modern" exhibition describes his 1955 doctoral dissertation as "the earliest major text on Abstract Expressionist painting."
100 Krauss's 1981 essay "The Originality of the Avant-Garde" offers a cogent account of Monet's quasi-industrial production strategies:

> On top of this constructed "instant," thin, careful washes of pigment establish the actual relations of color. Needless to say, these operations took—with the necessary drying time—many days to perform. But the illusion of spontaneity—the burst of an instantaneous, originary act—is the unshakeable result . . . The illusion of unrepeatable, separate instants is the product of a fully calculated procedure that was necessarily divided up into stages and sections and worked on piecemeal on a variety of canvases at the same-time, assembly-line style. Visitors to Monet's studio in the last decades of his life were startled to find the master of instantaneity at work on a line-up of a dozen or more canvases. (*Originality*, 167)

101 More recently, serial studies of water-towers and silos by photographers Bernd and Hilla Becher, of traffic intersections and

hotel atriums by Thomas Struth and Andreas Gursky, etc., confirm the continuing relevance of Monet's haystacks and cathedrals to late-twentieth-century reexaminations of abstract/representational binaries.

102 Here the broader New York School of poetry's integration into MoMA's early-sixties institutional culture does prove pertinent. By the time of Seitz's "Seasons and Moments" and "Assemblage" shows, Brainard's soon-to-be friends and collaborators Frank O'Hara and James Schuyler had been appointed Assistant Curator of Painting and Sculpture, and Curator of Circulating Exhibitions, respectively.

103 The cabinet (or closet) motif also has pointed significance, of course, within 1950s and early-60s queer New York culture, a predominantly domestic arena deftly described by poet/critic Wayne Koestenbaum:

> In the bleak McCarthy era, gay culture paradoxically flourished in the home—safer than police-threatened bars and tearooms. The private apartment—or townhouse—became a Joseph Cornell shadow box, a vitrine, an inside-out Brillo carton; in domiciles, queers amassed artworks, cleansers, masks, records, and receipts, with a curatorial intensity that Warhol would translate into an art of serial and repeated imagery, and into the collections (cookie jars, jewelry, superstars, drawings, cardboard-boxed time capsules) that were his signature, his incarceration, and his bid for immortality. (50)

104 More pertinent is Seitz's emphasis upon the crafty technological apparati employed by Monet:

> he began to utilize a slotted box containing several canvases of a given size from which, on returning to his motif from day to day, he could choose the one that best conformed to the light of the moment, continue working until the light changed (seldom more than half an hour), and replace it with another. (16)

For here, Monet's quasi-industrial painting process can be seen to serve (as it does in the Hal Foster and Rosalind Krauss passages quoted above) as part of a broader art-historical transition: from Impressionist plein-air excursions to the Warhol silkscreen Factory.

105 Once more, Krauss offers a concise account of how exaggerated praise for Monet's unmediated attunement to natural phenomena obscures his role as prolific producer of the modular part:

> as recent studies of Monet's impressionism have made explicit, the sketchlike mark, which functioned as the *sign* of spontaneity, had to be prepared for through the utmost calculation, and in this sense spontaneity was the most fakable of signifieds . . . [But] the discourse of originality in which impressionism participates represses and discredits the complementary discourse of the copy. (*Originality*, 167-168)

106 In a more recent manifestation of the phenomenon described above: Brainard's1975 Fishbach Gallery exhibition contains over 1500 artworks, selling for as little as twenty-five dollars each, as though geared to the spendthrift holiday-shopper (Padgett 222). After this successful show's offerings get dispersed, Brainard suffers his worst post-exhibition letdown to date, and never again exhibits. Here I hope to demonstrate, by analogy, how an oft-repeated bit of Brainard lore can take on broader art-literary-historical resonance—once placed amid a study of serial composition's self-obscuring tendencies.

107 Art-historian Benjamin Buchloh's "Andy Warhol's One-Dimensional Art" essay expands the concept of a "largest entity" within which to consider postwar serial composition—positioning Warhol's kitsch-affirming silk-screens as a critique of handmade high-art's dubious place within the postwar culture industry:

> Early on, [Warhol] seems to have understood that it would be the task of the new generations of artists to recognize and publicly acknowledge how far the conditions that allowed the formation of the abstract expressionist aesthetic along the parameters of romantic notions of heroic resistance and transcendental critique had actually been surpassed by the massive reorganization of society in the postwar period . . . This new civilization would create conditions in which mass culture and high art would be forced into an increasingly tighter embrace, leading to the integration of the sphere of high art into that of the culture industry . . . Purged of the political and

> ideological idea that artistic intervention in the social spheres of production and consumption would enable collective social progress, the cognitive and perceptual devices of modernity would have to be deployed simply for the development of a new commodity aesthetic (e.g., product design, packaging, and advertisement). (4-5)

108 Buchloh notes both Warhol's early successes in commercial design, and his subsequent popularity among his former patrons. Here the critic derides the "ever-increasing number of ad men who would become passionate collectors of avant-garde art (in order to buy off and embrace the 'creativity' that would perpetually escape them . . .)" (6).

109 Koestenbaum's reference to Warhol's less renowned, if no less provocative, critique of postwar art patronage (here in the form of commercial portraiture) suggests, once again, the blunting of a pointed serial project forced "underground":

> Warhol did fifty to one hundred of the commissioned portraits a year; many are privately owned, and unfortunately they may never be exhibited as a series. Imagined in their totality, however, they eviscerate the identity of each sitter, even as they pretend to perpetuate it . . . the joke was on the client: by being portrayed *as if* a Liz, the subject admitted an identity as stand-in, nonstar, aura seeker, just another flavor of person, without a monopoly on presence. (168)

110 For a quick introduction to Brainard's camp/constructivist mode of hermeneutic inquiry, see his *Twelve Postcards* (Calais, VT: Z Press, 1975).

111 Of course, within Brainard's own hybrid career, the artist/poet's collages, assemblages and paintings confirm his serial inclinations just as dramatically as does any literary text. For though the institutional norms of postwar art display (project-based gallery exhibitions for all but the best established living artists) generally encourage the creation of what might be called "series" (analogous to a company's latest product line), Brainard's intricate, all-over arrangements (of religious icons, flower paste-ons, tattoo decals, etc.) foreground a far more sophisticated examination of the serialized image.

112 For the sake of historical clarity, I here wish to cite critic Steven Watson's description of Warhol's earliest cloud sculpture as a "forty-foot tubular balloon that looked like a snake" (244). Subsequently, I will refer to Warhol's clouds in the plural, since the artist typically presented them in sets of smaller units.

113 As noted in this chapter's "Serial Instantaneity" section, Brainard provides an analogous offering two years prior, sacrificing his suntan-lotion prepped body to the "total gray clouds" of a buggy Vermont morning, with the hope that something better might come along ("You never can tell about Vermont, tho").

114 According to art-historian William Ganis, Warhol's Factory produced roughly 600 "unique stitched photographic objects" between 1982 (the year that Warhol's friend Christopher Makos proposed the idea) and Warhol's death in 1987 (24).

115 In his swift progression from Renaissance cloud to postwar serigraph, Barthes appears to hold in mind Warhol's 1966 Leo

Castelli Gallery show, an exhibition that combined the silver mylar clouds with the grid-like *Cow Wallpaper*:

> in many works of pop art, the background against which the object is silhouetted, or even out of which it is made, has a powerful existence (rather of the kind clouds had in classical painting): there is an importance of the grid. This comes, perhaps, from Warhol's first experiments: serigraphs depend on textile (textile and grid are the same thing); it is as if our latest modernity enjoys this manifestation of the grid, at once consecrating the raw material (grain of the paper in Twombly's work) and the mechanization of reproduction (micro-pattern of the computer portraits). (203)

116 In *A New Theory for American Poetry: Democracy, the Environment, and the Future of Imagination*, scholar Angus Fletcher sketches this hermeneutic affinity between Montaigne and Emerson:

> When Emerson wrote his "Circles," he was following in the footsteps of his formal master, Montaigne, whose late essay on three kinds of society, commerce, or association, as the word is variously translated, centered upon the description of his library: "The shape of my library is round with only sufficient flat wall for my table and chair; as it curves about, it offers me at a glance all my books arranged in five rows of shelves all around." (36)

Fletcher's analysis of spherical and/or architectural metaphors for the act of reading could extend back at least to Heraclitus' conception of *Logos* as (in Heidegger's terms) a "laying-before which gathers" (60). But within my present chapter it suffices to ask: What postwar image better fuses those of Emerson's circles and Montaigne's library than Warhol's wraparound "Campbell Soup Cans" display?

117 Brainard's hypothetically minded illustration "If Nancy was a Boy" (1972) will revisit the drinking-glasses' invitation to a below-the-waist unveiling, presenting Ernie Bushmiller's comic heroine with a pointy penis.

118 If my analysis of Warhol's clouds seems overdetermined, it here is worth considering that, according to Krauss, few pictorial tropes call for greater scrutiny:

> Perspective was thus understood from the first to be a matter of architectonics, of a structure built from delimited bodies standing in a specific space and possessing a contour defined by lines. The immeasurability and ubiquity of the sky, however, and the unanalyzable surfacelessness of the clouds render these things fundamentally unknowable by the perspective order . . . Thus before being a thematic element—functioning in the moral and allegorical sphere as a registration of miraculous vision . . . the /cloud/ is a differential marker in a semiological system. (*Bachelors*, 85)

Krauss bases this perspective-destabilizing analysis of "the / cloud/" upon Hubert Damisch's *Théorie du /nuage/* (Paris: Éditions du Seuil, 1972).

119 By extension, Brainard's late-sixties journals (such as "Diary 1969," quoted below) turn increasingly diffuse—comprised of fragmentary strophes, as though caught up in the centrifugal force that Warhol channels from his Factory rooftop:

> I *do* consider myself very much of an artist. But a real painter, no, not yet. I'm too spread out. And I'm just not that dedicated. That moral. But maybe I'm wrong. Or maybe I don't care much anymore. (true) True, at least, for today." (*Selected*, 63)

120 Along such lines, John Coplans has suggested that Warhol's "most decisive move" comes about through the rejection of "paint handling"—through the abandonment of dramatic, Ab Ex-derived brushstrokes, and the embrace of industrial process (silk-screened canvas, mass-produced mylar cloud, etc.) ("Early," 52). Similarly, I here posit that Brainard's most decisive move as serial poet takes place amid the progression from his early journals' narrative patina to *I Remember*'s anaphoric pulse:

> I decided one day that I would lay out in the sun and close my eyes and try to remember, and just write down whatever I remembered, free-floating . . . . . . But then I began to realize that beyond that point there is another level of knowledge that could be triggered off. It wasn't really useful knowledge unless it was triggered off. (Dlugos, 11)

Lying in the Vermont grass again (two years later this time), with the apogee of Pop pictorial innovation just behind him, Brainard remains committed to a "free-floating" poetic transcription, yet now with mechanized, serialized bent ("It isn't really there spontaneously") (Dlugos, 11). Conspicuous lyric "handling" yields to reflexive, propulsive "trigger."

121 In her gloss on the rhetorical conventions operative in James Wright's "Snowstorm in the Midwest," critic Marjorie Perloff sounds like Steiner discussing Alberti's *De Pictura*:

> The voice of the poem is solitary and speaks out of a single moment in time. (Perloff, *Dance* 155)

> In a painting with vanishing-point perspective and chiaroscuro, the assumption is that we are observing a scene through a frame from a fixed vantage point *at one moment in time*. (Steiner 23, the italics are Steiner's)

Both Perloff and Steiner, in fact, base their analyses of narrative upon *Critical Inquiry*'s Fall, 1980 special-issue on this theme.

122 Less strict than our chronological conception of history, less climactic than our catharsis-minded conception of story, Alberti's *istoria* suggests not a dramatic sequence of events, but a single, compacted scene ("beauty is born from the composition of planes") (Alberti, 72).

123 Brunelleschi's fifteenth-century biographer, Antonio Manetti, describes how the aforementioned architect composed his proto-perspective designs (and discovered that all lines converge

as they progress towards the horizon) by painting the reflected forms of buildings directly onto a mirror. Brainard's quasi-autobiographical assemblages, I have argued, use the "painted" (or, as in John Ashbery's poem, the "convex") mirror to equally compelling effect.

124 Georges Seurat offers an important transition: "Seurat, Van Gogh, and Cézanne built their compositions out of repeatable minimal units . . . But Seurat went on in *Les Poseuses* to repeat not only dots but his subject, who appears in three different poses on the same canvas" (Steiner, 5).

125 Steiner's imagined triptych evokes James Rosenquist's epic canvases, and thus suggests the diversity of aesthetic practices placed under the umbrella term "Pop." My own study, like Steiner's, focuses upon Pop's more serial-minded practitioners.

126 I take my reading of Lichtenstein's triptych from Steiner's adroit analysis (see *Pictures of Romance* pages 164-165).

127 Just as Warhol's serial display of each extant Campbell soup variety traces the constrictive circumference of consumerist choice, so his grid of sixteen Jackies appears to delimit the entire range of potential responses to personal and political trauma ("every" emotive possibility—as defined by the tabloid press).

128 Chatman's essay, "What Novels Can Do That Films Can't (And Vice Versa)," can be found in the Leo Braudy- and Marshall Cohen-edited anthology *Film Theory and Criticism*, 5th edition (Oxford: Oxford University Press, 1999).

129 Again, while Chatman's plot-minded definition of narrative might seem to exclude from attention Brainard's fragmentary text, it is this poet's autobiographical bent that grants many of his most

elliptical writings narrative status. For as Steiner here suggests, the implicit coherence assigned to autobiographical discourse permits increased deviation from classic dramatic paradigms:

> Its story wholeness, in the sense of its having a specific beginning, middle, and end, is an accomplished fact. Moreover, it already has a prototypical principle of story wholeness available to it—that of anyone's life. This "biographical model" is the totality that links countless medieval narrative paintings into wholes: the assumption of the central figure's life as the narrative that the episodes actually rendered demarcate. (32)

130 Within the twenty-first century, timely poetic projects such as the Claudia Rankine- and Juliana Spahr-edited anthology *American Women Poets in the 21st Century: Where Lyric Meets Language* (Middletown, Conn.: Wesleyan University Press, 2002) have sought to contest such strict dichotomies.

131 Again I take my analysis of this painting from Steiner (see *Pictures of Romance* pages 28-29).

132 Krauss's 1978 essay "Grids" juxtaposes images by Odilon Redon and Piet Mondrian in order to suggest that at the "radical" modernist grid's origins lies the "retrograde" Symbolist window.

133 Though Perloff's "From Image to Action" piece does refer to Cage as a "narrative poet," this essay never employs Cage's narrative-based texts to further its own critique of last-gasp variants on the "paradigmatic modernist lyric" (*Dance* 156). Perloff's 1981 collection, *The Poetics of Indeterminacy: Rimbaud to Cage*, more-

over, does offer an extended analysis of Cage's individual stories, yet remains largely indifferent to the *Indeterminacy* project as a distinct, self-governing whole. As a result, many macro-compositional complexities of Cage's performance-based script get lost amid a far more general approach to "the Cagean story," combined with a sequence of close readings—myopic attempts to articulate the "didactic" ethos of individual entries (inevitably, that the story/the world is "absurd") (*Poetics* 315). Between these definitional pronouncements and interpretive minutiae, little room remains to consider Cage's fusion of affective increment and all-over composition, of camp parable and Pop sequence.

134 French novelist Georges Perec (himself a Brainard emulator, as suggested by 1978's *Je me souviens*) will further refine this vision in his *Life: A User's Manual*—a book whose narrative conceit, Perec-confidant Harry Mathews tells us, was "originally suggested by a Saul Steinberg drawing," and required that its author "imagine a nine-story, turn-of-the-century Parisian apartment building from which the facade has been removed" (Mathews, 5).

135 Less sleek than the streamlined urban skyscraper, Brainard's incremental edifice includes more nooks and crannies, more eroticized, Benozzo-esque dens and foyers:

> I remember locker rooms. And locker room smells. (49)
>
> I remember a dark green cement floor covered with wet footprints going in all different directions. Thin white towels. And not "looking around" too much. (50)

> I remember fantasies of being in jail, and very monk-like in my cell, hand-writing out a giant great novel. (96)
>
> I remember (on the other hand) fantasies of being in jail, and of good raw sex. All very "black and white" somehow. Black bars, white tiles. White flesh, black hairs. The rubbery warm whites of cum, and the shiny cold blacks of leather and slate. (96)

I remember a sex fantasy sequence in my head of being forced to "perform" on the floor, under the stairs, of an apartment building I either lived in, or was visiting, I can't remember which. Needless to say, the mad sex fiend criminal rapist was pretty cute to boot. (106)

WORKS CITED

Albers, Josef. "The Origin of Art." *Theories and Documents of Contemporary Art: A Sourcebook of Artists' Writings.* Eds. Kristine Stiles and Peter Selz. Berkeley: University of California Press, 1996. 107.

Alberti, Leon Battista. *On Painting.* 1435. Translated by John R. Spencer. New Haven: Yale University Press, 1956.

Alloway, Lawrence. "Popular Culture and Pop Art." *Studio Intenational* (July-August) 1969: 17-21.

Apollinaire, Guillaume. "La Petite Auto." *Calligrammes: Poems of Peace and War.* 1918. Trans. Anne Hyde Greet. Berkeley: University of California Press, 1980. 104.

Ashbery, John. *Selected Prose.* Ed. Eugene Richie. Ann Arbor: University of Michigan Press, 2004.

Ashton, Jennifer. "Sincerity and the Second Person: Lyric after

Language Poetry." *Interval(le)s* II.2-III.1 (Fall 2008/Winter 2009); 94-108.

Barrett, Ed. "The Living End." *Pressed Wafer* 2 (March 2001):144-148.

Berrigan, Anselm. "I remember hearing Joe read." *Pressed Wafer* 2 (March 2001): 212.

Boaden, James. "San Francisco, Ruin of the Nineteenth Century: The Assemblage Work of Bruce Conner, 1957 – 1962." *Papers of Surrealism* 2 (Summer 2004): 1-19.

Barthes, Roland. Barthes, Roland. *Camera Lucida: Reflections on Photography*. 1981. New York: Hill and Wang, 1990.

—. "Day by Day with Roland Barthes." Trans. Richard Howard. *On Signs*.

Ed. Marshall Blonsky. Baltimore: Johns Hopkins University Press, 1985. 98-117.

—. *The Responsibility of Forms: Critical Essays on Music, Art, and Representation*. Trans. Richard Howard. 1985. Berkeley: University of California Press, 1991.

—. *Roland Barthes*. Trans. Richard Howard. New York: Hill and Wang, 1977.

Baudelaire, Charles. *Poems*. Trans. Roy Campbell. New York: Pantheon Books, 1952.

Beckett, Tom. Interview with Susan Howe. *Difficulties* 3.2 (1989): 17-27.

Benjamin, Walter. "The Author as Producer." Trans. Edmund Jephcott. *Selected Writings*. Vol. 2. Eds. Marcus Bullock and Michael W. Jennings. Cambridge, Mass: Belknap Press, 1996-2003.

Bernstein, Charles. *Girly Man*. Chicago: University of Chicago Press 2006.

Bidart, Frank. *In the Western Night: Collected Poems, 1965-90.* New York: Farrar Straus Giroux, 1990.

Bochner, Mel. "The Serial Attitude." *Artforum* (December 1967) 28-33.

Bockris, Victor. *Transformer: The Lou Reed Story*. New York: Simon and Schuster, 1995.

Brainard, Joe. *Bolinas Journal*. Bolinas, CA: Big Sky Books, 1971.

—. "Frank O'Hara." *Homage to Frank O'Hara*. 1978. Eds. Bill Berkson and Joe LeSueur. Bolinas, CA: Big Sky, 1988.

—. *I Remember*. New York: Angel Hair, 1970.

—. *I Remember*. New York: Full Court Press, 1975.

—. *I Remember More*. New York: Angel Hair, 1972.

—. *New Work*. Los Angeles: Black Sparrow Press, 1971.

—. *Nothing to Write Home About*. Los Angeles: Little Caesar Press, 1981.

—. *Selected Writings: 1962-1971*. New York: Kulchur Foundation, 1971.

Brown, Lee Ann. "Joe Acrostics." *Pressed Wafer* 2 (March 2001): 221.

Buchloh, Benjamin. "Andy Warhol's One-Dimensional Art: 1956-1966." *Andy Warhol*. Ed. Annette Michelson. Cambridge, Mass: MIT Press, 2001. 1-48.

Cage, John. *Silence: Lectures and Writings*. 1961. Cambridge, Massachusetts: The M.I.T. Press, 1970.

—. *M: Writings: '67-'72*. Middletown, Conn: Wesleyan University Press, 1973.

—. *A Year from Monday; New Lectures and Writings*. Middletown, Conn: Wesleyan University Press, 1967.

Caws, Mary Ann. *Manifesto: A Century of Isms*. Lincoln: University of Nebraska Press, 2001.

Chernoff, Maxine. "Sonnet: Some Things I Miss About Joe." *Pressed Wafer* 2 (March 2001): 128-129.

Clark, Tom. "My Joe Brainards." *Pressed Wafer* 2 (March 2001): 98-100.

Coleridge, Samuel Taylor. *Coleridge's Criticism of Shakespeare*. Ed. R.A. Foakes. Detroit: Wayne State University Press, 1989.

Conte, Joseph. *Unending Design: The Forms of Postmodern Poetry*. Ithaca: Cornell University Press, 1991.

Coolidge, Clark. *Space*. New York, Harper & Row, 1970.

Coplans, John. *Serial Imagery*. Pasadena, CA: Pasadena Art Museum, 1968.

—. "Early Warhol: The Systematic Evolution of the Impersonal Style." *Artforum* 8.2 (March 1970): 52-55.

—. *Reclining Figure, Two Panels, No. 1*. 1996. Reprinted from www.nationalgalleries.org.

Corbett, William. Introduction to "Hello Joe" Tribute. *Pressed Wafer* 2 (March 2001): 85-87.

—. "Seventeen Titles Joe Brainard Will Use One Day." *L=A=N=G=U=A=G=E* 3.11 (January 1980): 12-13.

Crimp, Douglas. "Spacious." *October* 132 (Spring 2010): 5-24.

Davidson, Michael. *Guys Like Us: Citing Masculinity in Cold War Politics*.Chicago:TheUniversityofChicagoPress,2004.Dickinson, Emily. *The Complete Poems of Emily Dickinson*.Ed. Thomas H. Johnson. 1960. Boston: Little, Brownand Company. 1961.

Dlugos, Tim. "Starting with Nothing and Surprising Himself: the Joe Brainard Interview." *Little Caesar* 10 (1980). Condensed version reprinted in *The James White Review* 18.1 (Spring 2001)

4-17.

Elderfield, John. "Grids," *Artforum* (May 1972): 52-59.

Emerson, Ralph Waldo. *Journals of Ralph Waldo Emerson with Annotations*. Eds. Edward Waldo Emerson and Waldo Emerson Forbes. New York: Houghton Mifflin, 1991.

Fletcher, Angus. *A New Theory for American Poetry: Democracy, the Environment, and the Future of Imagination*. Cambridge, Mass: Harvard University Press, 2004.

Foster, Hal. *The Return of the Real: The Avant-Garde at the End of the Century*. Cambridge, Mass: MIT Press, 1996.

Foucault, Michel. *Archaeology of Knowledge*. 1969. Trans. A.M. Sheridan Smith. New York: Routledge, 1972.

Ganis, William. *Andy Warhol's Serial Photography*. New York: Cambridge University Press, 2004.

Gooch, Brad. "Nancy Ideas." *Artforum* (February 2001): 124-128.

Greenberg, Clement. *The Collected Essays and Criticism: Modernism with a Vengeance, 1957-1969*. Vol. 3. Ed. John O'Brian. Chicago: University of Chicago Press. 1986.

—. "Modernist Painting." *Twentieth Century Theories of Art*. Ed. James M. Thompson. 1990. Ottawa: Carleton University Press, 1999. 94-101.

Hainley, Bruce. "I Remember." *Frieze* 9 May 1996: Frieze Foundation Archive. Reprinted from www.frieze.com.

Heidegger, Martin. *Early Greek Thinking*. Trans. David Farrell Krell and Frank A. Capuzzi. New York: Harper & Row, 1975.

Hejinian, Lyn. *My Life*. Los Angeles: Sun and Moon Press, 1987.

Howe, Susan. Howe, Susan. *Frame Structures: Early Poems, 1974-1979*. New York: New Directions, 1996.

—. *Singularities*. Middletown, CT: Wesleyan University Press, 1990. Reprinted with the permission of Wesleyan University Press.

Jabès, Edmund. "To Be in the Book." *Manifesto: A Century of Isms*. Ed. Mary Ann Caws. Lincoln: University of Nebraska Press, 2001. 679-680.

Koestenbaum, Wayne. *Andy Warhol*. New York: Viking, 2001.

—. *Cleavage: Essays on Sex, Stars, and Aesthetics*. New York: Ballantine Books, 2000.

Kostelanetz, Richard. *John Cage (ex)plain(ed)*. New York: Schirmer Books, 1996.

Krauss, Rosalind. *Bachelors*. Cambridge, Mass: MIT Press, 1999.

—. *The Originality of the Avant-Garde and Other Modernist Myths*. Cambridge, Mass: MIT Press, 1985.

Lee, David. "Serial Rights." *Art News* 66.8 (December 1967): 42-45, 68-69.

Lehman, David. *The Last Avant-Garde: The Making of the New York School of Poets*. New York: Doubleday, 1998.

Leonardo. *Annunciation*. 1472-1475. *Uffizi Gallery*, Florence. Re printed from www.artchive.com

Mallarmé, Stéphane. *Selected Poetry and Prose* Ed. Mary Ann Caws. New York: New Directions, 1982.

Marinetti, Fillipo Tommaso. *Après la Marne, Joffre visita le front en auto. Manifesto: a Century of Isms*. Ed. Mary Ann Caws. Lincoln: University of Nebraska Press, 2001. 190.

Mathews, Harry. "That Ephemeral Thing." *The New York Review of Books* 16 June, 1988. Reprinted from www.nybooks.com.

Matthiessen, Francis Otto. *American Renaissance: Art and Expression in the Age of Emerson and Whitman*. 1941. New York: Oxford

University Press, 1968.
McCaffery, Steve. "The Death of the Subject." *L=A=N=G=U=A=G=E* Supplement Number One (June 1980); 2-18.
—. *North of Intention: Critical Writings, 1973-1986.* New York: Roof Books, 1986.
McHale, Brian. *Postmodernist Fiction.* New York, Methuen, 1987.
Moss, Howard. *Minor Monuments: Selected Essays.* New York: Ecco Press, 1996.
Myles, Eileen. *Chelsea Girls.* Santa Rosa, CA: Black Sparrow Press, 1994.
Nietzsche, Friedrich. *Basic Writings of Nietzsche.* Trans. Walter Kaufmann. New York: Modern Library, 1968.
—. *The Gay Science.* Trans. Walter Kaufmann. New York: Vintage Books, 1974.
O'Hara, Frank. *The Collected Poems of Frank O'Hara.* Ed. Donald Allen. 1971. Berkeley: University of California Press, 1995.
Oldenburg, Claes. *Store Days: Documents from The Store, 1961, and Ray Gun Theater, 1962.* New York: Something Else Press, 1967.
Park, Darragh. "Jottings for a letter sent to Joe while he was in the hospital the last six months of his illness." *Pressed Wafer* 2 (March 2001): 202-203.
Padgett, Ron. *Joe: A Memoir of Joe Brainard.* Minneapolis: Coffee House Press, 2004.
Perloff, Marjorie. *The Dance of the Intellect: Studies in the Poetry of the Pound Tradition.* 1985. Evanston: Northwestern University Press, 1996.
—. *Differentials: Poetry, Poetics, Pedagogy.* Tuscaloosa: University of Alabama Press, 2004.

—. "'a duchamp unto my self': 'writing through' Marcel." *John Cage: Composed in America*. Eds. Marjorie Perloff and Charles Junkerman. Chicago: University of Chicago Press, 1994. 100-122.

—. *Frank O'Hara: Poet among Painters*. 1977. Chicago: University of Chicago Press, 1997.

—. "How to Read a Poem: W.B. Yeats's 'After Long Silence.'" 2007. Reprinted from www.marjorieperloff.com.

—. *The Poetics of Indeterminacy: Rimbaud to Cage*. 1981. Evanston, Ill: Northwestern University Press, 1999.

—. *Poetry on & off the Page: Essays for Emergent Occasions*. Evanston, Ill: Northwestern University Press, 1998.

—. *Radical Artifice: Writing Poetry in the Age of Media*. Chicago: University of Chicago Press, 1991.

Poe, Edgar Allen. *Essays and Reviews*. New York: Library Classics of the United States, 1984.

—. *Poems and Tales*. New York: Literary Classics of the United States, Inc., 1984

Quartermain, Peter. Rev. of *Unending Design: The Forms of Postmodern Poetry*, by Joseph Conte. *American Literature* 64. 2 (June 1992): 413-414.

Raphael. *The School of Athens*. 1510-1511. Apostolic Palace, Vatican City. Reprinted from www.ancientworlds.com.

Ratcliff, Carter. "Attending to the Ordinary." *Art in America* 85 (July 1997): 72-77.

Reinhardt, Ad. *Art as Art: The Selected Writings of Ad Reinhardt*. Ed. Barbara Rose. New York: Viking Press, 1975.

Rosenberg, Harold. *The Tradition of the New*. 1960. New York: De Capo Press, 1994.

Rosenblum, Robert. Introduction. *Art in the Age of Aquarius:*

1955-1970. By William Chapin Seitz. Ed. Marla Prince. Washington: Smithsonian Institution Press, 1982.

—. *On Modern American Art: Selected Essays*. New York: Harry A. Adams, 1999.

—. "Pop Art and Non-Pop Art." *Art and Literature* (Summer 1965): 80-93.

Sappho. "Fragment 102." Trans. Moreton John Walhouse. *The Sappho Companion*. Ed. Margaret Reynolds. New York: Palgrave, 2001. 57.

Saussure, Ferdinand de. *Course in General Linguistics*. New York: Philosophical Library, 1959.

Schuyler, James. *Collected Poems*. New York: Farrar Straus Giroux, 1993.

—. Book cover. *Hand over Heart: Poems 1981-1988*. By David Trinidad. New York: Amethyst Press, 1991.

Seitz, William Chapin. *The Art of Assemblage*. New York: Museum of Modern Art, 1961.

—. *Claude Monet: Seasons and Moments*. 1960. New York: Arno Press, 1969.

Silliman, Ron. *The Age of Huts (Compleat)*. Berkeley: University of California Press, 2007.

—. "For Open Letter." *L=A=N=G=U=A=G=E* Supplement Number One (June 1980); 30-34.

Smithson, Robert. *The Collected Writings*. Ed. Jack Flam. Berkeley: University of California Press, 1996.

Sontag, Susan. *Against Interpretation and Other Essays*. 1966. New York: Anchor Books, 1990.

Steiner, Wendy. *Pictures of Romance: Form against Context in Painting and Literature*. Chicago: University of Chicago Press, 1988.

Thomson, Virgil. "Cage and the Collage of Noises." *American Music since 1910*. Ed. Virgil Thomson. New York: Holt, Rinehart, and Winston, 1971. 67-81.

Trinidad, David. "Joe Brainard Pink." *Pressed Wafer* 2 (March 2001): 166.

—. *Plasticville*. Chappaqua, NY: Turtle Point Press, 2000.

Turner, Victor. "Social Dramas and Stories About Them." *On Narrative*. Ed. W.J. Thomas Mitchell. Chicago, University of Chicago Press, 1981. 137-164.

Warhol, Andy & Pat Hackett. *The Philosophy of Andy Warhol: from A to B and Back Again*. San Diego: Harcourt Brace Jovanovich, 1975.

—. *POPism: The Warhol '60s*. 1980. San Diego: Harcourt Brace Jovanovich, 1990.

Warsh, Lewis. *Avenues of Escape*. Brooklyn, NY: Long News Books, 1995.

—. "Joe Brainard." *Pressed Wafer* 2 (March 2001): 109-110.

Watson, Steven. *Factory Made: Warhol and the Sixties*. New York: Pantheon Books, 2003.

White, Edmund. *The Burning Library: Essays*. New York: Knopf, 1994.

—. "Saint Joe." *Art in America* (July 1997): 78-81.

Whitman, Walt. *Complete Poetry and Collected Prose*. New York: Literary Classics of the United States, 1982.

Wittgenstein, Ludwig. *Tractatus Logico-Philosophicus*. Trans. D.F. Pears & B.F. McGuinness. New York: Humanities Press, 1961.

Wolf, Reva. *Andy Warhol, Poetry, and Gossip in the 1960s*. Chicago: University of Chicago Press, 1997.

Image Acknowledgments

Figure 1, page 25: Joe Brainard
Ultra-New Realism Self-Portrait 1972
graphite on paper and collage, 13 x 10 1/2
Courtesy of Joe Brainard Collection, Mandeville Special Collections Library, UC San Diego.

Figure 4, page 62: Susan Howe, excerpt from "Thorow," from *Singularities* © 1990 by Susan Howe. Reprinted with permission of Wesleyan University Press.

Figure 5, page 148: IA1994.13
Andy Warhol (American, 1928-1987)
Silver Clouds [Warhol Museum Series], 1994

Helium-filled metalized plastic film (Scotchpak)
Flat: 35 x 52 in. (88.9 x 132.1 cm.)
Inflated: 32 x 48 x 15 in. (81.3 x 121.9 x 38.1 cm.)
The Andy Warhol Museum, Pittsburgh.

Figure 6, page 154: 1998.1.2683
Andy Warhol (American, 1928-1987)
Unidentified Male, 1986
gelatin silver prints sewn with thread
27 ½ x 21 3/8 in. (69.9 x 54.3 cm.)
The Andy Warhol Museum, Pittsburgh; Founding Collection, Contribution The Andy Warhol Foundation for the Visual Arts, Inc.

Figure 9, page 167: 1939.1.293
Master of the Osservanza (Sano di Pietro?)
The Meeting of Saint Anthony and Saint Paul
c. 1430/1435
tempera on panel
painted surface: 46.5 x 33.4 cm (18 5/16 x 13 1/8 in.)
overall: 47 x 33.6 cm (18 ½ x 13 ¼ in.)
framed: 61.6 x 125.4 x 7.6 cm (24 ¼ x 49 3/8 x 3 in.)
Samuel H. Kress Collection

Image courtesy of the National Gallery of Art, Washington

Figure 10, page 169: 1968.2
Andy Warhol
Sixteen Jackies
1964
acrylic, enamel on canvas
80-3/8 x 64-3/8", 81-7/16 x 65-5/16 x 2-1/8" installed
Collection Walker Art Center, Minneapolis
Art Center Acquisition Fund, 1968

Figure 11, page 170: Roy Lichtenstein
As I Opened Fire Poster, 1966
© Estate of Roy Lichtenstein

Figure 12, page 181: 1952.2.3
Benozzo Gozzoli
The Feast of Herod and the Beheading of Saint John the Baptist
1461-62
tempera (?) on panel
overall: 23.8 x 34.5 cm (9 3/8 x 13 9/16 in.)
framed: 40.3 x 50.6 x 4.4 cm (15 7/8 x 19 15/16 x 1 ¾ in.)
Samuel H. Kress Collection
Image courtesy of National Gallery of Art, Washington

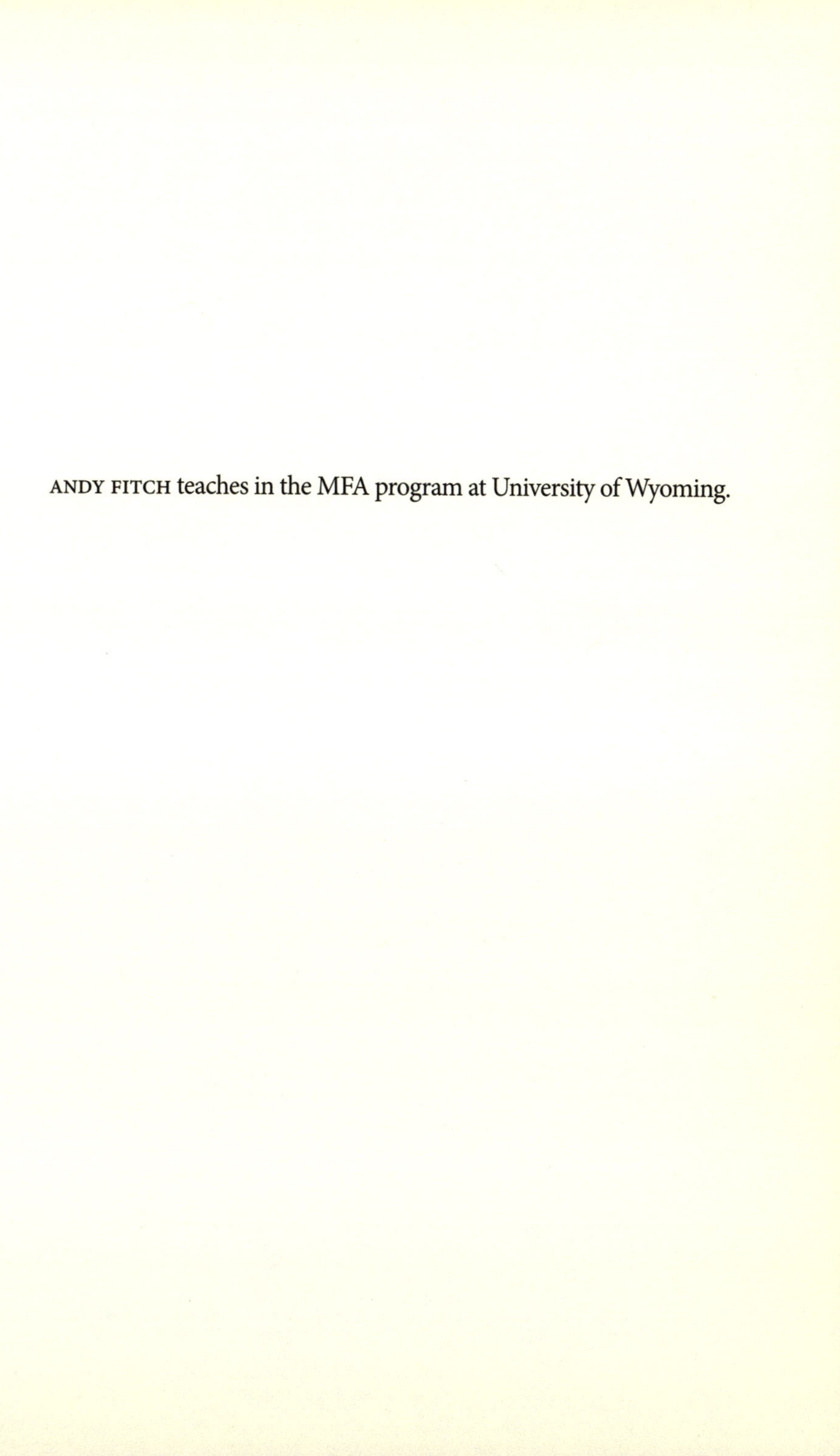

ANDY FITCH teaches in the MFA program at University of Wyoming.

SELECTED DALKEY ARCHIVE TITLES

Petros Abatzoglou, *What Does Mrs. Freeman Want?*
Michal Ajvaz, *The Golden Age.*
The Other City.
Pierre Albert-Birot, *Grabinoulor.*
Yuz Aleshkovsky, *Kangaroo.*
Felipe Alfau, *Chromos.*
Locos.
João Almino, *The Book of Emotions.*
Ivan Ângelo, *The Celebration.*
The Tower of Glass.
David Antin, *Talking.*
António Lobo Antunes, *Knowledge of Hell.*
The Splendor of Portugal.
Alain Arias-Misson, *Theatre of Incest.*
Iftikhar Arif and Waqas Khwaja, eds., *Modern Poetry of Pakistan.*
John Ashbery and James Schuyler, *A Nest of Ninnies.*
Robert Ashley, *Perfect Lives.*
Gabriela Avigur-Rotem, *Heatwave and Crazy Birds.*
Heimrad Bäcker, *transcript.*
Djuna Barnes, *Ladies Almanack.*
Ryder.
John Barth, *LETTERS.*
Sabbatical.
Donald Barthelme, *The King.*
Paradise.
Svetislav Basara, *Chinese Letter.*
Miquel Bauçà, *The Siege in the Room.*
René Belletto, *Dying.*
Marek Bieńczyk, *Transparency.*
Mark Binelli, *Sacco and Vanzetti Must Die!*
Andrei Bitov, *Pushkin House.*
Andrej Blatnik, *You Do Understand.*
Louis Paul Boon, *Chapel Road.*
My Little War.
Summer in Termuren.
Roger Boylan, *Killoyle.*
Ignácio de Loyola Brandão,
Anonymous Celebrity.
The Good-Bye Angel.
Teeth under the Sun.
Zero.
Bonnie Bremser, *Troia: Mexican Memoirs.*
Christine Brooke-Rose, *Amalgamemnon.*
Brigid Brophy, *In Transit.*
Meredith Brosnan, *Mr. Dynamite.*
Gerald L. Bruns, *Modern Poetry and the Idea of Language.*
Evgeny Bunimovich and J. Kates, eds., *Contemporary Russian Poetry: An Anthology.*
Gabrielle Burton, *Heartbreak Hotel.*
Michel Butor, *Degrees.*
Mobile.
Portrait of the Artist as a Young Ape.
G. Cabrera Infante, *Infante's Inferno.*
Three Trapped Tigers.
Julieta Campos,
The Fear of Losing Eurydice.
Anne Carson, *Eros the Bittersweet.*
Orly Castel-Bloom, *Dolly City.*
Camilo José Cela, *Christ versus Arizona.*
The Family of Pascual Duarte.
The Hive.
Louis-Ferdinand Céline, *Castle to Castle.*
Conversations with Professor Y.
London Bridge.
Normance.
North.
Rigadoon.
Marie Chaix, *The Laurels of Lake Constance.*
Hugo Charteris, *The Tide Is Right.*
Jerome Charyn, *The Tar Baby.*
Eric Chevillard, *Demolishing Nisard.*
Luis Chitarroni, *The No Variations.*
Marc Cholodenko, *Mordechai Schamz.*
Joshua Cohen, *Witz.*
Emily Holmes Coleman, *The Shutter of Snow.*
Robert Coover, *A Night at the Movies.*
Stanley Crawford, *Log of the S.S. The Mrs Unguentine.*
Some Instructions to My Wife.
Robert Creeley, *Collected Prose.*
René Crevel, *Putting My Foot in It.*
Ralph Cusack, *Cadenza.*
Susan Daitch, *L.C.*
Storytown.
Nicholas Delbanco, *The Count of Concord.*
Sherbrookes.
Nigel Dennis, *Cards of Identity.*
Peter Dimock, *A Short Rhetoric for Leaving the Family.*
Ariel Dorfman, *Konfidenz.*
Coleman Dowell,
The Houses of Children.
Island People.
Too Much Flesh and Jabez.
Arkadii Dragomoshchenko, *Dust.*
Rikki Ducornet, *The Complete Butcher's Tales.*
The Fountains of Neptune.
The Jade Cabinet.
The One Marvelous Thing.
Phosphor in Dreamland.
The Stain.
The Word "Desire."
William Eastlake, *The Bamboo Bed.*
Castle Keep.
Lyric of the Circle Heart.
Jean Echenoz, *Chopin's Move.*
Stanley Elkin, *A Bad Man.*
Boswell: A Modern Comedy.
Criers and Kibitzers, Kibitzers and Criers.
The Dick Gibson Show.
The Franchiser.
George Mills.
The Living End.
The MacGuffin.
The Magic Kingdom.
Mrs. Ted Bliss.
The Rabbi of Lud.
Van Gogh's Room at Arles.
François Emmanuel, *Invitation to a Voyage.*
Annie Ernaux, *Cleaned Out.*
Salvador Espriu, *Ariadne in the Grotesque Labyrinth.*
Lauren Fairbanks, *Muzzle Thyself.*
Sister Carrie.
Leslie A. Fiedler, *Love and Death in the American Novel.*
Juan Filloy, *Faction.*
Op Oloop.
Andy Fitch, *Pop Poetics.*
Gustave Flaubert, *Bouvard and Pécuchet.*
Kass Fleisher, *Talking out of School.*

FOR A FULL LIST OF PUBLICATIONS, VISIT:
www.dalkeyarchive.com

SELECTED DALKEY ARCHIVE TITLES

Ford Madox Ford,
The March of Literature.
Jon Fosse, *Aliss at the Fire.*
Melancholy.
Max Frisch, *I'm Not Stiller.*
Man in the Holocene.
Carlos Fuentes, *Christopher Unborn.*
Distant Relations.
Terra Nostra.
Vlad.
Where the Air Is Clear.
Takehiko Fukunaga, *Flowers of Grass.*
William Gaddis, *J R.*
The Recognitions.
Janice Galloway, *Foreign Parts.*
The Trick Is to Keep Breathing.
William H. Gass, *Cartesian Sonata and Other Novellas.*
Finding a Form.
A Temple of Texts.
The Tunnel.
Willie Masters' Lonesome Wife.
Gérard Gavarry, *Hoppla! 1 2 3.*
Making a Novel.
Etienne Gilson,
The Arts of the Beautiful.
Forms and Substances in the Arts.
C. S. Giscombe, *Giscome Road.*
Here.
Prairie Style.
Douglas Glover, *Bad News of the Heart.*
The Enamoured Knight.
Witold Gombrowicz,
A Kind of Testament.
Paulo Emílio Sales Gomes, *P's Three Women.*
Karen Elizabeth Gordon, *The Red Shoes.*
Georgi Gospodinov, *Natural Novel.*
Juan Goytisolo, *Count Julian.*
Exiled from Almost Everywhere.
Juan the Landless.
Makbara.
Marks of Identity.
Patrick Grainville, *The Cave of Heaven.*
Henry Green, *Back.*
Blindness.
Concluding.
Doting.
Nothing.
Jack Green, *Fire the Bastards!*
Jiří Gruša, *The Questionnaire.*
Gabriel Gudding,
Rhode Island Notebook.
Mela Hartwig, *Am I a Redundant Human Being?*
John Hawkes, *The Passion Artist.*
Whistlejacket.
Elizabeth Heighway, ed., *Contemporary Georgian Fiction.*
Aleksandar Hemon, ed.,
Best European Fiction.
Aidan Higgins, *Balcony of Europe.*
A Bestiary.
Blind Man's Bluff
Bornholm Night-Ferry.
Darkling Plain: Texts for the Air.
Flotsam and Jetsam.
Langrishe, Go Down.
Scenes from a Receding Past.
Windy Arbours.
Keizo Hino, *Isle of Dreams.*
Kazushi Hosaka, *Plainsong.*
Aldous Huxley, *Antic Hay.*
Crome Yellow.
Point Counter Point.
Those Barren Leaves.
Time Must Have a Stop.
Naoyuki Ii, *The Shadow of a Blue Cat.*
Mikhail Iossel and Jeff Parker, eds.,
Amerika: Russian Writers View the United States.
Drago Jančar, *The Galley Slave.*
Gert Jonke, *The Distant Sound.*
Geometric Regional Novel.
Homage to Czerny.
The System of Vienna.
Jacques Jouet, *Mountain R.*
Savage.
Upstaged.
Charles Juliet, *Conversations with Samuel Beckett and Bram van Velde.*
Mieko Kanai, *The Word Book.*
Yoram Kaniuk, *Life on Sandpaper.*
Hugh Kenner, *The Counterfeiters.*
Flaubert, Joyce and Beckett: The Stoic Comedians.
Joyce's Voices.
Danilo Kiš, *The Attic.*
Garden, Ashes.
The Lute and the Scars
Psalm 44.
A Tomb for Boris Davidovich.
Anita Konkka, *A Fool's Paradise.*
George Konrád, *The City Builder.*
Tadeusz Konwicki, *A Minor Apocalypse.*
The Polish Complex.
Menis Koumandareas, *Koula.*
Elaine Kraf, *The Princess of 72nd Street.*
Jim Krusoe, *Iceland.*
Ayşe Kulin, *Farewell: A Mansion in Occupied Istanbul.*
Ewa Kuryluk, *Century 21.*
Emilio Lascano Tegui, *On Elegance While Sleeping.*
Eric Laurrent, *Do Not Touch.*
Hervé Le Tellier, *The Sextine Chapel.*
A Thousand Pearls (for a Thousand Pennies)
Violette Leduc, *La Bâtarde.*
Edouard Levé, *Autoportrait.*
Suicide.
Mario Levi, *Istanbul Was a Fairy Tale.*
Suzanne Jill Levine, *The Subversive Scribe: Translating Latin American Fiction.*
Deborah Levy, *Billy and Girl.*
Pillow Talk in Europe and Other Places.
José Lezama Lima, *Paradiso.*
Rosa Liksom, *Dark Paradise.*
Osman Lins, *Avalovara.*
The Queen of the Prisons of Greece.
Alf Mac Lochlainn,
The Corpus in the Library.
Out of Focus.
Ron Loewinsohn, *Magnetic Field(s).*
Mina Loy, *Stories and Essays of Mina Loy.*
Brian Lynch, *The Winner of Sorrow.*
D. Keith Mano, *Take Five.*
Micheline Aharonian Marcom,
The Mirror in the Well.
Ben Marcus,
The Age of Wire and String.

SELECTED DALKEY ARCHIVE TITLES

Wallace Markfield,
Teitlebaum's Window.
To an Early Grave.
David Markson, *Reader's Block.*
Springer's Progress.
Wittgenstein's Mistress.
Carole Maso, *AVA.*
Ladislav Matejka and Krystyna Pomorska, eds.,
Readings in Russian Poetics: Formalist and Structuralist Views.
Harry Mathews,
The Case of the Persevering Maltese: Collected Essays.
Cigarettes.
The Conversions.
The Human Country: New and Collected Stories.
The Journalist.
My Life in CIA.
Singular Pleasures.
The Sinking of the Odradek Stadium.
Tlooth.
20 Lines a Day.
Joseph McElroy,
Night Soul and Other Stories.
Thomas McGonigle,
Going to Patchogue.
Robert L. McLaughlin, ed., *Innovations: An Anthology of Modern & Contemporary Fiction.*
Abdelwahab Meddeb, *Talismano.*
Gerhard Meier, *Isle of the Dead.*
Herman Melville, *The Confidence-Man.*
Amanda Michalopoulou, *I'd Like.*
Steven Millhauser, *The Barnum Museum.*
In the Penny Arcade.
Ralph J. Mills, Jr., *Essays on Poetry.*
Momus, *The Book of Jokes.*
Christine Montalbetti, *The Origin of Man.*
Western.
Olive Moore, *Spleen.*
Nicholas Mosley, *Accident.*
Assassins.
Catastrophe Practice.
Children of Darkness and Light.
Experience and Religion.
A Garden of Trees.
God's Hazard.
The Hesperides Tree.
Hopeful Monsters.
Imago Bird.
Impossible Object.
Inventing God.
Judith.
Look at the Dark.
Natalie Natalia.
Paradoxes of Peace.
Serpent.
Time at War.
The Uses of Slime Mould: Essays of Four Decades.
Warren Motte,
Fables of the Novel: French Fiction since 1990.
Fiction Now: The French Novel in the 21st Century.
Oulipo: A Primer of Potential Literature.
Gerald Murnane, *Barley Patch.*
Inland.
Yves Navarre, *Our Share of Time.*
Sweet Tooth.
Dorothy Nelson, *In Night's City.*
Tar and Feathers.
Eshkol Nevo, *Homesick.*
Wilfrido D. Nolledo, *But for the Lovers.*
Flann O'Brien, *At Swim-Two-Birds.*
At War.
The Best of Myles.
The Dalkey Archive.
Further Cuttings.
The Hard Life.
The Poor Mouth.
The Third Policeman.
Claude Ollier, *The Mise-en-Scène.*
Wert and the Life Without End.
Giovanni Orelli, *Walaschek's Dream.*
Patrik Ouředník, *Europeana.*
The Opportune Moment, 1855.
Boris Pahor, *Necropolis.*
Fernando del Paso, *News from the Empire.*
Palinuro of Mexico.
Robert Pinget, *The Inquisitory.*
Mahu or The Material.
Trio.
A. G. Porta, *The No World Concerto.*
Manuel Puig, *Betrayed by Rita Hayworth.*
The Buenos Aires Affair.
Heartbreak Tango.
Raymond Queneau, *The Last Days.*
Odile.
Pierrot Mon Ami.
Saint Glinglin.
Ann Quin, *Berg.*
Passages.
Three.
Tripticks.
Ishmael Reed, *The Free-Lance Pallbearers.*
The Last Days of Louisiana Red.
Ishmael Reed: The Plays.
Juice!
Reckless Eyeballing.
The Terrible Threes.
The Terrible Twos.
Yellow Back Radio Broke-Down.
Jasia Reichardt, *15 Journeys Warsaw to London.*
Noëlle Revaz, *With the Animals.*
João Ubaldo Ribeiro, *House of the Fortunate Buddhas.*
Jean Ricardou, *Place Names.*
Rainer Maria Rilke, *The Notebooks of Malte Laurids Brigge.*
Julián Ríos, *The House of Ulysses.*
Larva: A Midsummer Night's Babel.
Poundemonium.
Procession of Shadows.
Augusto Roa Bastos, *I the Supreme.*
Daniël Robberechts, *Arriving in Avignon.*
Jean Rolin, *The Explosion of the Radiator Hose.*
Olivier Rolin, *Hotel Crystal.*
Alix Cleo Roubaud, *Alix's Journal.*
Jacques Roubaud, *The Form of a City Changes Faster, Alas, Than the Human Heart.*
The Great Fire of London.
Hortense in Exile.
Hortense Is Abducted.
The Loop.
Mathematics:
The Plurality of Worlds of Lewis.

FOR A FULL LIST OF PUBLICATIONS, VISIT:
www.dalkeyarchive.com

SELECTED DALKEY ARCHIVE TITLES

The Princess Hoppy.
Some Thing Black.
Leon S. Roudiez, *French Fiction Revisited.*
Raymond Roussel, *Impressions of Africa.*
Vedrana Rudan, *Night.*
Stig Sæterbakken, *Siamese.*
Lydie Salvayre, *The Company of Ghosts.*
Everyday Life.
The Lecture.
Portrait of the Writer as a Domesticated Animal.
The Power of Flies.
Luis Rafael Sánchez, *Macho Camacho's Beat.*
Severo Sarduy, *Cobra & Maitreya.*
Nathalie Sarraute, *Do You Hear Them?*
Martereau.
The Planetarium.
Arno Schmidt, *Collected Novellas.*
Collected Stories.
Nobodaddy's Children.
Two Novels.
Asaf Schurr, *Motti.*
Christine Schutt, *Nightwork.*
Gail Scott, *My Paris.*
Damion Searls, *What We Were Doing and Where We Were Going.*
June Akers Seese, *Is This What Other Women Feel Too?*
What Waiting Really Means.
Bernard Share, *Inish.*
Transit.
Aurelie Sheehan, *Jack Kerouac Is Pregnant.*
Viktor Shklovsky, *Bowstring.*
Knight's Move.
A Sentimental Journey: Memoirs 1917–1922.
Energy of Delusion: A Book on Plot.
Literature and Cinematography.
Theory of Prose.
Third Factory.
Zoo, or Letters Not about Love.
Claude Simon, *The Invitation.*
Pierre Siniac, *The Collaborators.*
Kjersti A. Skomsvold, *The Faster I Walk, the Smaller I Am.*
Josef Škvorecký, *The Engineer of Human Souls.*
Gilbert Sorrentino, *Aberration of Starlight.*
Blue Pastoral.
Crystal Vision.
Imaginative Qualities of Actual Things.
Mulligan Stew.
Pack of Lies.
Red the Fiend.
The Sky Changes.
Something Said.
Splendide-Hôtel.
Steelwork.
Under the Shadow.
W. M. Spackman, *The Complete Fiction.*
Andrzej Stasiuk, *Dukla.*
Fado.
Gertrude Stein, *Lucy Church Amiably.*
The Making of Americans.
A Novel of Thank You.
Lars Svendsen, *A Philosophy of Evil.*
Piotr Szewc, *Annihilation.*
Gonçalo M. Tavares, *Jerusalem.*
Joseph Walser's Machine.
Learning to Pray in the Age of Technique.
Lucian Dan Teodorovici, *Our Circus Presents . . .*
Nikanor Teratologen, *Assisted Living.*
Stefan Themerson, *Hobson's Island.*
The Mystery of the Sardine.
Tom Harris.
Taeko Tomioka, *Building Waves.*
John Toomey, *Sleepwalker.*
Jean-Philippe Toussaint, *The Bathroom.*
Camera.
Monsieur.
Reticence.
Running Away.
Self-Portrait Abroad.
Television.
The Truth about Marie.
Dumitru Tsepeneag, *Hotel Europa.*
The Necessary Marriage.
Pigeon Post.
Vain Art of the Fugue.
Esther Tusquets, *Stranded.*
Dubravka Ugresic, *Lend Me Your Character.*
Thank You for Not Reading.
Tor Ulven, *Replacement.*
Mati Unt, *Brecht at Night.*
Diary of a Blood Donor.
Things in the Night.
Álvaro Uribe and Olivia Sears, eds., *Best of Contemporary Mexican Fiction.*
Eloy Urroz, *Friction.*
The Obstacles.
Luisa Valenzuela, *Dark Desires and the Others.*
He Who Searches.
Marja-Liisa Vartio, *The Parson's Widow.*
Paul Verhaeghen, *Omega Minor.*
Aglaja Veteranyi, *Why the Child Is Cooking in the Polenta.*
Boris Vian, *Heartsnatcher.*
Llorenç Villalonga, *The Dolls' Room.*
Toomas Vint, *An Unending Landscape.*
Ornela Vorpsi, *The Country Where No One Ever Dies.*
Austryn Wainhouse, *Hedyphagetica.*
Paul West, *Words for a Deaf Daughter & Gala.*
Curtis White, *America's Magic Mountain.*
The Idea of Home.
Memories of My Father Watching TV.
Monstrous Possibility: An Invitation to Literary Politics.
Requiem.
Diane Williams, *Excitability: Selected Stories.*
Romancer Erector.
Douglas Woolf, *Wall to Wall.*
Ya! & John-Juan.
Jay Wright, *Polynomials and Pollen.*
The Presentable Art of Reading Absence.
Philip Wylie, *Generation of Vipers.*
Marguerite Young, *Angel in the Forest.*
Miss MacIntosh, My Darling.
REYoung, *Unbabbling.*
Vlado Žabot, *The Succubus.*
Zoran Živković, *Hidden Camera.*
Louis Zukofsky, *Collected Fiction.*
Vitomil Zupan, *Minuet for Guitar.*
Scott Zwiren, *God Head.*